To Then and Back Again

To Then and Back Again

A Memoir Part One A Collection of Uh-Oh's, No No's and A Few OMG'S

JERRY BRYSON MCMILLAN

ARPress
ILLUMINATING IDEAS
EMPOWERING VOICES

ARPress LLC
45 Dan Road Suite 5
Canton MA 02021
Hotline: 1(888) 821-0229
Fax: 1(508) 545-7580

Ordering Information:
Quantity sales. Special discounts are available on quantity purchases by corporations, associations, and others. For details, contact the publisher at the address above.

Printed in the United States of America.

ISBN-13:	Softcover	979-8-89330-079-6
	Hardcover	979-8-89330-080-2
	eBook	979-8-89330-081-9

Library of Congress Control Number: 2024902460

Contents

Preface

My name is Jerry McMillan. I'm now in my mid-forties and have few regrets about my life. I've done good things, bad things, and things I wish I could just forget. However, and in all honesty, I like who I am, and those things I've done, tried, or didn't try are what makes me who I am ... and I'm finally comfortable with this person I call me. I must admit, though, I've had one small desire for quite some years now, and if you are reading this, then I've reached my goal.

It's been over ten years since I began writing my story. However, my intentions have morphed over the years from wanting to tell my mother's story, which I thought was quite interesting, to telling my story, which I feel is equally interesting. Hopefully, this book will bear the fruits of my labors and experiences well as you continue reading. I, too, hope, if only for a short while, that it will allow you to walk in another's shoes and to gaze at the world through another's eyes—albeit eyes that are now a little weary.

When I began writing my book, I was consumed and wrote feverishly for about three months. Then a peculiar thing happened. It would seem that I found another purpose for writing other than the gratification of telling a story. I found it quite therapeutic and genuinely liberating; it was as if in my writing I had thrown off the yoke of self-denial with which I had so regrettably adorned through the years. However, the story I would have told then is nothing like the one I'm writing today.

My original writings were much more dark, morose, and sophomoric to a degree. Back then, I was searching my soul for the most miserable, vile, and despicable things that had happened in my life. I wanted to cut them out like an ugly cancer and didn't care if it was with scalpel precision or butcher knife crudeness. I just wanted the disease out so I could throw the whole mess onto paper and then offer it with pride and glory to the world as the story of my worthless, self-loathing life. But in accepting the person I was, the person I now am, this wasn't to be.

I believe that I'd unintentionally freed myself from the chaos I so dearly wanted to write about, and in coming to grips with my own self, I felt the writing experience had served its purpose, so I put down the book. I wasn't so interested in writing anymore, it seemed. But I've always known I have this wonderful and sometimes unbelievable story to tell; something to say to everyone, but not preachy, you know. To wit, the writing bug had bitten again, and I've paid it some serious attention this time.

Looking back, I can see how immature a person and a writer I was, whereas today, I believe I am sufficiently mature and capable of telling my story irrespective of the consequences of laying my soul bear for the entire world to see, only this time without the shame and stigma I might have felt had I done so back then.

In essence, I really wasn't as sure of myself or my own intentions, but I'm now ready to start anew; I've picked the book back up, dusted it off, and will tell my story in all its candor; in all its wonder; and in all its distaste, but with the dignity it deserves, and without the shame and pain I had endured for so many years, so long ago.

Today, I'm not a rich man, a man of importance, or fame. I'm not known for doing anything great. I suppose I'm only known to my own circle of friends and family, and even then, it's only as an average Joe scientist guy whose profession involves writing about all sorts of scientific and technical matters and developing new products.

I am, however, a Joe who has an extraordinary story to tell. A story that might seem to meander in the beginning but will surely elicit great emotion and wonder ... and possibly even a touch of disbelief, but God willing, it will always keep you, the reader, fascinated and wanting more.

As you continue reading, it might seem that some of the stories are too fantastic or fanciful to be real, but I assure you this is not the case. These are many of my real-life experiences, and through them all, I have, in one way or another, dealt with each in my own fashion as they came along. Maybe not always perfectly, but in the best way I knew how.

I have only written about those richest, most interesting details concerning my life ... or so I would like to think. I will sometimes digress as I narrate, but only to enhance the experience I'm trying to relay. And, too, there are some things that I would not write about today and maybe never will write about, but that discussion and subsequent decision is certainly left for another day.

Today, however, I can only hope that I am adept enough to sufficiently move beyond my scientific milieu to illustrate and convey these sometimes simple, sometimes complex, but many times emotionally charged experiences I've had.

Whether these emotions were elicited by the harsh realities of adversity that I, like many, have faced and overcome or by the personal triumphs achieved through perseverance, and at times, through sheer willpower alone, I can't necessarily discern. I will, however, try to express them in such a manner as to allow you, the reader, the chance to decide for yourself.

So, let's now embark on a journey to then and back again, an odyssey that will encompass a multitude of adventures that are, at times, disturbing and chaotic and, at other times, fascinating and humorous. These adventures will range from overcoming desperation and loneliness as a result of a hidden identity to the anguish of a best friend and his suicide that served absolutely no purpose nor had any meaning; a suicide that gained nothing for anyone ... especially himself. From an insidious monster's theft of a child's innocence to things that just happen, catching you unaware, then kicks you square in your pearly whites.

The journey, my friend, will certainly run the gamut of human experiences and emotions, and I'm willing to share them if you wish to take the ride. During this ride, they will vicariously become your adventures as well.

However, because I've had so many 'adventures' in my life, in fact, I could probably write about them for the rest of my life, I've decided to write them in a two-part series with the first part consisting of my young childhood and teenage years, and the second part consisting of my young adult life until just after I moved on from the town I once called home.

Life is a gift to be cherished, learned from, and used up before moving on. But remember, as given in Donne's Prose, meditation 17: "Any man's death diminishes me because I am involved in mankind; and therefore, never send to know for whom the bell tolls; it tolls for thee ..."

Prologue

The Family

Four brothers comprise the McMillan boys: Chris, Tom, Myself, and Albert, from oldest to youngest. We were all born in different states and about three years apart. This was because our dad was in the Air Force and was stationed all over the country but did quite a few tours of duty overseas; Chris was born in Bangor, Maine; Tom was born in Amarillo, Texas; I was born in Champaign, Illinois; and I think Albert was born in Enid, Oklahoma ... Yep, pretty sure it was Enid.

Mom, God rest her soul, always said the only time she ever got pregnant was when dad came home on leave from overseas, which was apparently about every three years. I don't know if this is true, and I never particularly wanted to confirm it ... it just makes for a nice little story I will remember all my life.

Chris was born in 1956. He favors our dad in the looks department. He was as normal as a kid could be, not really excelling in anything but popularity—with the women, that is, not really as a jock. He was the best-looking of all of us. The women loved him, and the men envied him; I, of course, never realized this until I was older.

He played sports, but I never paid attention to sports until I was in Junior High. Chris would have been a senior in high school then, so I don't know if he was any good at sports. I suppose since we were all athletic to some degree, so was he.

He's done pretty well for himself and his family over the years and has been married for 30 years or so with two kids and two grandkids. I believe he and his family are a happy lot, or as happy as anyone can be in this life, but I'm sure, as with most, he feels he could have done more.

I've always respected him, but there have been a few times I felt a lot of animosity toward him, but I overcame my problems with him, and today we are great friends. In the end, he's my brother, and as with the other two, I love him regardless of our past differences, and that's what brothers are for, aren't they? To love and stick up for one another through thick and thin?

To this day, I credit him as having the coolest head in the family and the hardest to upset or agitate (unless it's politics and ... Wow! He can be an animal). He doesn't have the passion for arguing or fighting that the rest of us do. Again, this was how our dad was, and he has the same temperament.

Since both our parents have passed on, Chris has taken on the role of the family Patriarch. I know this because he sometimes tends to act not only as a brother but as a father when he feels it necessary to dispense advice.

He can be challenging sometimes, but I know whatever he thinks, says, or does as it concerns us brothers, it's only because he cares and wants what's best for us even though all of us are in our forties or fifties these days. But to this day, I credit Chris with saving my life on one occasion and my legs on another, and will never forget it.

Then there's Tom. Tom was born in 1960. Dad used to brag about how he thought Tom was the smartest of all of us and would amount to the most. This, of course, was before Tom started goofing up his life; first by running away, then one continual screw-up after another during his life. Dad just couldn't understand how one so bright could be so misguided. I guess he wasn't thinking about how his and Mom's alcoholism could have played a roll.

And truthfully, Tom is very bright, but Dad never realized that not only did our family's dysfunction play a role in his less than stellar life, but also how later on, other, more menacing, and appalling things also played a grim role.

Tom and I were probably more alike growing up than the other two brothers because not only were we the two middle children, but we were also both into, and good at, sports. I competed for many of Tom's Junior High and High school track records back then and took quite a few of them from him, but didn't take them all, which would have been just plain rude and a little un-brotherly of me now, wouldn't it?

He has three kids, one who's an adult and two who are still teenagers, and so although he has always been in a precarious situation, at least he has children. Concerning Tom, after reading my memoirs, if you think I've had problems in my life, they pale compared to this guy's problems. Maybe his life and times will be my next project.

Then there's me. I was born in 1963. I wasn't the brightest of the bunch, as I was the devil's child. When I showed up, rest assured, trouble was around the corner. I never had to look for trouble as it always seemed to find me.

Mom used to tell me and everyone else that I could clear a room just by walking in. I got the belt more than all three brothers put together, and sometimes it wasn't pretty. I was constantly getting into trouble, and I believe if it hadn't been for my mother's 'tough love'—I mean, really tough love—and her iron grip, I would not be the man I am today ... good, bad, or indifferent.

I remember one time in third grade when I was about eight years old. I got into trouble with my teacher, Mrs. Hargraves. My punishment was to stay after school, where I had to sit in my chair without talking. While sitting there, she went to the office to do something or other. After leaving the room, I noticed she'd left her purse next to her desk.

Being the snoopy little scamp I was, and without missing a beat, I went over to it and looked inside. While rummaging through it, I noticed an envelope that contained about twenty dollars.

The money was the proceeds from the book club she'd collected from all her students. Not thinking 'right or wrong,' I reached in and grabbed it, feeling I had just collected a great booty that would bring me lots of happiness in the near future.

This was a Friday, so the next morning, I decided to go to the town Sundry. I bought snacks and a trinket or two for myself but became bored. I decided to go find a few friends and tell them to come with me as I was treating; telling them I had some money I had saved and wanted to spend it with them.

I bought all sorts of stuff, whatever they asked for, as long as it wasn't too spendy. This gave me the feeling of sincere pleasure as I recall; that I was able to do this kind of thing for my friends for the first time ever in my life felt great. However, a kid back then and at the age of about eight shouldn't have twenty bucks … especially to blow, and spending it at the local drug store would certainly attract attention, and it did.

Wilma Baxter, who was working the counter that day, must have thought it a little odd as she was ringing up everything I was buying for myself and my buddies. Little did I know she would contact my mom once I left, and also that Mrs. Hargraves had discovered the missing money and called Mom the very same day. Talk about sucking at being a thief.

When I got home later that afternoon, I found there would be hell to pay for my wrongdoing, as Mom always said she couldn't abide thieves or liars. No sooner than she began grilling me did it all come out; I told her everything because I really sucked at lying as well. That's when she did the first, worst thing she had ever done to me. She took me into the bathroom and whipped me like a rented mule.

After she'd finished whipping the white right off my back, she ran a bath and put me in the tub. I don't recall whether or not she drew blood, but I know it welted badly. She then walked to the toilet across the bathroom and plopped down as if it was a magnet, and her butt was made of steel.

She sobbed for what seemed an eternity. I soon began crying, too, because I knew it'd hurt her so much to do what she did and that it was me who had caused her to cry. So, you see, Mom was very 'proactive' when it came to her children thieving, and as you'll see in another chapter, she doesn't like liars either and is just as proactive then, as well.

Once she regained her composure, she dressed me and marched me out to Mrs. Hargraves' house with the twenty dollars I owed. I returned the money I'd stolen, of which ten was still left after my spending spree, and I apologized for my wrongdoing.

Marcia, Mrs. Hargraves, forgave me and asked me to never do it again, to which I agreed. I do want to say here that my mother never physically abused me out of simply being abusive. She just didn't know how to control me, except by punishing me the way she did; the way she had been punished when she was a child, only not near to the degree she had been.

I hold no ill will or grudge toward her at all, and to be honest, it seemed that eventually, it took hold ... once I became too big to whip. I was a decent, respectable student once I reached High school. I got decent grades and, for the most part, stayed away from trouble. I would like to think that I was, and still am, a good and decent person because of my upbringing and my own sense of right and wrong.

I honestly believe that what she did never had a lasting negative effect on me. I also believe that, to a large degree, it was partly because of her I didn't become someone who is either antisocial or, worse, a psychopathic wacko. I have my problems, as we all do, but being perfect is not being human, and I think we all like to consider ourselves humans.

Today, I work as a scientist managing the Technical Services and Product Research and Development departments of a small pharmaceutical company in Omaha, Nebraska, and I am doing fairly well for myself, and I guess I can give thanks that things turned out for the better rather than for the worse.

Albert was the youngest and was born in 1966. He was Mom's little baby. He was coddled more than all of us, and she doted over him when he was younger and cared for him until she passed on when he was about 30 years old. Although to hear him speak of them, he hated them for what he felt they did to him—again, I refer back to the dysfunctionality of our family.

He feels he was treated horribly as a child, especially by Dad. He also feels that during his darkest times, when my parents were at their worst, us brothers abandoned him and left him to his own devices. I'm not going to try and dispute this, but rather, I'm going to let Albert have his demons from the past. However, he's the one who has to wrestle with them and is the only one who can exorcise them from his mind, heart, and soul.

Albert was a thin and spindly child. He had long platinum silver hair that Mom loved and women envied. Mom kept it cropped like a Dutch boy, only way longer; straight bangs with the sides and back flowing down a little past his shoulders and all of it as straight as an arrow.

He was a very fair-skinned kid whose naturally blonde hair would bleach to a silvery white during the summer. It was quite a site, but it made him look like a little girl as you watched him walk away or saw him from afar. Albert was just a normal kid like Chris, Tom, and I, and not much bad going on until he got a little older after the fire.

I know he had issues growing up, and he blames his brothers, along with his parents, for many of the troubles that have befallen him, but again, it will take a lot more time for you to discover the Albert I know.

He currently works for Chris and lives from day to day, which is fine, as that's what he chooses, and I've come to accept it. Suffice it to say, he is our brother, and we love him, but sometimes—many times—he can be exasperating.

Joyce was our mother. She passed on in 1996 at the age of 64. She was a real humdinger of a woman who hailed from the mountains of Tennessee. She was a true tomboy at heart who was fiercely protective of her kids and family, so it was best not to cross her, whether you were in the right or wrong.

However, if she defended you and found out you were in the wrong, it probably would have been better just to let her not defend you to begin with—this was just how she operated. She was five-one and weighed a whopping hundred pounds soaking wet, but you didn't want to cross her because she was a real scrapper and didn't back down regardless of size.

I recall an incident when we lived in the garage of an old red brick house in Solomon. Albert had been about 12 or so at the time and had been playing a game of dungeons and dragons with his friends. They were all upstairs, just left of the hall's stairwell. I was lying in bed reading but could see and hear everything as it played out.

Mom had yelled up the stairs asking Albert to come down and take out the trash. Well, you know kids, he never listened to Mom, especially on the first request. She again yelled at him and again, no answer. Then it was silent for a while, as if she just stopped asking. Then it happened. Mom was at the top of the stairs as if appearing out of thin air. There was no warning at all for poor Albert or his friends. She had her broom in hand and yelled, "Boy, you'd better get down the stairs and take out that damn trash!"

Albert then made the first, worst mistake he could possibly make at that moment; he told her, "In a minute, Mom," and the fight was on.

Apparently, she'd had enough of his disobedience. I leaned out of my bed and could see the anger on her face. She was fuming. Then with the accuracy of a laser-guided missile, she took the broom handle and landed a whack directly on his head.

No sooner than the row occurred, the other kids jumped up and out of the way for fear they would get whacked as well. Then with the smooth dexterity of a cat, she came around the table, inflicting one rap after the other upon his poor noggin and anywhere else he was protecting.

He was trying to guard his head with his hands, but she was true to her mark and, like a swashbuckling pirate, kept whacking and parrying as if he were her foe and had to be beaten. She continued her attack as Albert never agreed to comply with her demand.

Within seconds after laying about five or so blows on him, he jumped up from the chair, yelling for her to quit, screaming, "Stop it, STOP, MOM!" But his pleas were to no avail as she flew around the table after him.

In another couple of seconds, I saw him looking at me as if begging me to come to his rescue. That wasn't happening, though, because I knew if I did, my ass would get it just as bad, if not worse.

His eyes then darted toward my window, which was open and, luckily, without a screen. Instantly, he began his escape and charged quickly through my door. As he got to the window, he turned to see she was in hot pursuit and not far behind. He looked quickly at me, then took a look down and, in a split second, jumped from my window to the ground in front of the house.

No sooner had he jumped than Mom was at the window looking down. She yelled at him to stop, but without hesitation, she shot out the window herself. I freaked. I jumped up to the window to watch the scene emerging below.

Albert had just gotten up from a crouched position where he had landed with a dull thud. In an instant, Mom landed right behind him. Had he immediately taken off running, he could have escaped without much problem, but he paused instead, which was his mistake.

He had miscalculated mom's agility and her tom-boy-type nerves of steel; honestly, she stuck the landing quite well. But regardless of that, I'm sure he was in as much shock and awe as I was at that particular moment.

After the thud and the realization of what was happening, he turned around only to find mom about three feet away. Startled, he took off running, but she was right on his ass.

It was crazy and comical all at once and a moment I will relish forever. Albert did get away, but he had to come home eventually, and … well, I'll let your imagination figure out what happened then.

And so, my friend, this is another little glimpse into the many-faceted sides of my mother. And, too, I'm sure you will feel the same about her as I did and still do, as you continue reading. She surely was one crazy lady.

In recounting this story, Albert told a slightly different version of it this past Christmas. Although his version was slightly different, it was just as funny and, to some degree, quite poignant.

In doing the corroborating research for my memoir, I've come to realize it's all about time and each person's perception as we all remember things from so long ago just a little differently, but that's okay as the story is still real, only slightly skewed from person to person.

And finally, there's our dad, George. Dad was an absent father during most of our childhood years. It seemed he was only a provider for the first nine years or so of my life because he was a military man who served in the Air Force for twenty-something years and was always being transferred around the country.

However, once the children started school, they decided to set down roots. Although we were already living in Solomon, they decided to buy a home where we could live and flourish.

After retiring from the Air Force, Dad had gone to work harvesting for his friend, Don Hargraves, during the summer. This was because he wanted to retire from the Air Force, but because he was so young at 39, he didn't want to retire completely.

Don had a harvest crew that followed the wheat harvests from the south early on in the year to the north as the summer progressed and the crops became ready. So, this would get Dad out of the house for a few months out of the year and still give him something to do, I suppose.

It had been Mom's job to raise us for most of the time we were growing up. When Dad retired from the Air Force and began spending time with us boys, I believe Mom became a little protective and even a little jealous of Dad when he began actively participating in our rearing. Therefore, Mom didn't particularly care for his correcting and disciplining us, and she made it abundantly clear that it wasn't his job because he wasn't around before, so there was no need to start now.

I heard her tell him this many times and would countermand his authority when he did try to correct us. Eventually, this would stop as we grew older, but at the time, it put a hell of a strain on their marriage and our family.

Dad had put a lot of responsibility on Mom as far as our rearing was concerned. I suppose since his mother raised a large brood, he thought it would be an easy job for Mom to do as well. He probably didn't understand, or realize that his mother had five children by her first husband, my grandfather, then four more by her second husband, my great uncle; after my grandfather died, she married granddad Mac's brother.

When you think about it, Dad's new half-brothers and sisters were actually his first cousins as well … Odd, huh? Or, to look at it another way, four of my aunts and uncles are actually my cousins as well. Think about that one for a minute. Or another way … my dad is my second cousin by marriage—even weirder.

The first brood, which included two boys and three girls, was obviously grown enough to take care of the second brood, which included two boys and two girls. It isn't so far-fetched to think it would be difficult to bring up nine children, but ma'am ma Mac didn't work most of the time and had a full-time husband around for both sets of children. However, nine kids is still a hell of a brood to support and rear over the years, even with the help of the older children.

Our dad wasn't a really emotional man at all and was very calm in most cases. But when Mom got him all worked up, and they would fight like cats and dogs, it was never a pleasure to watch them going at it.

I remember walking into one of these little 'rituals' when I was probably fourteen. I have no idea what started it, and when it was finished, I never asked. All I know is that when I walked up to the front door one night, I heard yelling and screaming. I peeked through the front window to find Dad running back and forth across the living room, yelling for her to stop.

Mom was standing at the other end of the room where she had a buffet separating the dining area from the living room. She was shelling him with all the dinnerware she could get her hands on: plates, saucers, cups—it was all good. She was calling him a son of a bitch, all the while lobbing one artillery shell after another. I don't think she ever hit him through, or she surely would have inflicted some serious damage.

I know that most men would have walked out on her after something like this, but like they were, and like he was, he threatened but never did. I'll never know why, but that was just how he was, and that was how their relationship had always been. This lasted until about five years before Dad passed on when they became how they should have been all along: cool, collected, and respectful to one another.

So now you've basically met the family, and be assured you will read more about them as we go through the years of my life. I will also introduce you to many people; friends I've had forever and friends who have come and gone.

It is interesting how all of these incidents and adventures tend to intersect and how these people intertwine, sometimes for the good and sometimes ... well, not so much. But they are part of me and who I am, and I'm mostly grateful and far richer for ever having them in my life.

The House

The home that Mom and Dad decided to settle down in was a large, white, single-story Victorian with a large open attic. It was probably built sometime at the turn of the nineteenth century. It had a large gray porch that ran the length of the front. There was no railing to enclose the porch, only four large posts—one on each end and one on each side of the steps.

The steps were large, too, about six or seven feet wide, and made of concrete; the size was necessary because it was a large porch that sat about three feet up from the ground. Were they any smaller, they would have been dwarfed by the porch, making them look quite odd.

The front door was made of well-worn, old oak. It had a large oval-shaped beveled lead glass window that ran most of the door's height; it was quite remarkable and beautiful in its own right.

The house sat on a very sturdy foundation of concrete blocks painted gray like the porch. Each block must have weighed at least thirty or more pounds. Their shape and construct were not the typical flat, rectangular shape of haydite or cinder blocks used today. These were the old, solid core type, each having one side in the shape of a baguette-style cut gem.

The baguette-style cut is when a girdle is cut around one of the rectangular sides of the stone at an angle of approximately forty-five degrees. The angle then leads to the table leaving about eighty percent of the area of the original surface. The difference between the gem cut and the concrete block cut is that the table's surface of the block is not smooth but is rather uneven with a rough texture. I've recently found the concrete blocks to be quite pleasing architecturally, and so I have probably spent more time than necessary in their description.

The home's exterior was typical of the architectural style of the period. The roof had three gables, each with a full-sized window in its middle. The largest gable was located at the front end of the roof ridge or front of the house. The roof's eaves and the porch roof line created the triangle for the front gable.

The two side gables were located on opposing sides of the roof ridge, adjacent to one another, and centered along the length of the home. These, however, didn't run the entire length of the sides of the house because the roof's backside was hipped rather than gabled. The roof's eaves formed the bottom lines of the two side gables' triangles.

All three gables then comprised the area of the attic. So, with the entirety of these opposing gables, one can only imagine how angular the walls and roof lines of the attic must have been. Nevertheless, this was good since the design would make for some very interesting architecture once Dad remodeled it into bedrooms. Unfortunately, this never came to pass due to the tragedy that would befall our family late one summer night not long after beginning our new life, yet so long ago from my current life.

The only other architecturally significant structures of the home were the large, floor-to-ceiling bay windows, one in the living room and the other in the family room. They were really quite impressive as the ceilings were around twelve feet tall. Unfortunately, all the oak woodwork that framed the windows and trimmed the floors and doorways were painted white, and it would take a lot of time and energy to strip and refinish all of it, which was one of Mom's projects on her 'to-do' list.

The kitchen was an addition to the home and was really quite large, as it ran the entire length of the back of the home. As I recall, the siding was also a wider lapboard than the rest of the home. The kitchen was much more modern than the rest of the home, so it had probably been added sometime in the near past.

Large windows all along the back of the kitchen gave a mostly unobstructed view of the backyard. I believe what we called the family room had been the original kitchen, and when the previous owners added the new kitchen, they had used the old kitchen for their dining room. However, because the kitchen was so large, we didn't need a dining room, so we used it for the family room.

As you walked into the kitchen from outside, the dining table was just to the right, and a large chest-type deep freezer sat to the left. The far end of the kitchen included the cabinets, sink, and appliances, all of which formed a tidy U shape.

Dad had finished remodeling the kitchen, and one of his accomplishments was a beautiful built-in China hutch he had crafted. The piece wasn't unusually ornate but was very well crafted; straight lines, oak shelves and trim, and glass front doors with fine knobs and hinges. It was a very solid and quite interesting piece of cabinetry.

There was something quite peculiar about its construction, though. The basement door had been located in the kitchen, which he removed and then built the cabinet inside the door frame; it was much larger than the doorway but still about the same height and about four feet wide on the outside. The inside, however, was just a bit smaller than the width of the door frame, and it was about twelve inches deep.

He had engineered it so that when it was gently pulled, it would swing out before opening to the left, creating a hidden door that was covered by this large China cabinet. It was even more dramatic when it opened as you were staring at this gaping black hole. Only the first few steps were scarcely illuminated, so it appeared to be a staircase heading down into endless nothingness.

In retrospect, it reminds me of one of those old movies where the actors find a hidden passageway behind a wooden panel in an old castle that was lost somewhere in time. Once the panel is opened, it leads down into a musty and dark hall with precious little light to lead the way. Then, when you come to the end of the passage, you are in a cold and dark dungeon where you might spend the rest of your life alone. In reality, however, what lay at the bottom of these stairs was, of course, not an old dungeon but rather the old dirt floor of an old damp basement.

The basement had been where my older brothers, Tom and Chris, would take target practice with a semiautomatic 0.22 caliber rifle, which will feature prominently in a later chapter. They had also created an escape passage through a small window; for what reason, I have no idea. It led just outside, but when Dad discovered it, he was none too happy.

I don't remember much about it because I was usually too scared to go down there by myself. There wasn't anything for me down there anyway. Tom and Chris never invited me as I would have been like a wet blanket who only put a damper on their fun, or alternatively, maybe thought I would snitch them out for what they were doing should they let me know about it. It wasn't until I discussed this with Tom did I even realize that's what they were doing.

Now, Dad wasn't the only one with a flair for interior design. I remember when Mom began one of her 'projects.' Her first update was to redo the family room, and for some reason, she decided to begin with the floor. To let you know, her design sense—or maybe just her decorating tastes—were a little bizarre; at about eight years old, I watched her commit a colossal *faux pas* that caused what was, without doubt, a decorating disaster, which any eight-year-old, let alone adult, would have noticed.

The family room had been covered in old, badly worn linoleum, probably laid back in the thirties or forties. Mom, of course, being fearless about many things, of which trying new things was one, decided rather than just ripping up the old linoleum and laying down tile or carpet, she would experiment a little.

With all her decorating knowledge and interior design acumen, she decided to paint the floor. Of course, she told nobody what she was going to do, but rather decided to surprise everyone ... and surprise she did ... it nearly brought tears to my eyes at first and then laughter I could barely contain, but contain I did.

As far as I am aware, there was no such thing as linoleum floor paint back then, but this was not to deter her ambition. She didn't even pick the color out herself as some old paint had been left over from some other project from who knows when.

How insane is that? I now have to believe she wasn't a spendthrift because she apparently thought splurging on a five-dollar gallon of paint might have broken the bank. It was an awful, deep hunter-green, high gloss paint glaring a garish lime color when the light shone on it just right.

I'll never forget coming home from school that day. I walked into the kitchen, and just as I headed into the family room to go to my bedroom, she yelled, "Stop! The paint is still wet!"

I stopped just before turning to step into the room, and as soon as I did, I looked down at the floor, and my gaze became transfixed as my jaw hit the floor; I was in total disbelief. I was horrified, yet at once mesmerized. Even at that age, all I could do was roll my mind's eyes ... around and around and tell her almost apologetically how nice it looked ... all the while screaming in my head—Oh my God, yuk! Yuk! Yuk!

I have to believe all those who ever got a look at it in its entire, shocking splendor were really too kind—really—and never spoke about how they honestly felt. I'm sure some were indifferent, but if anyone liked it, they had no taste whatsoever.

To this day, I have no idea where I got my design or decorating sense, not that I have much, but thankfully, it wasn't from her. And I just want to say that I'm not trying to diss my mother, just showing another of her many-faceted sides.

I know she only meant well, and it is not as big a deal today as it was when I was a child. Honestly, though, I didn't want any of my friends coming over because of this, but eventually, we all became used to it, but never, ever whispered a word about what we really thought.

During the summer, the place to be was out on the back lawn. The City swimming pool was essentially in our backyard, just across the alley to which the backyard was adjacent. Mom, Dad, and all of us kids were very fond of it because they could use it as a babysitter but still keep an eye on us while we had fun swimming; great summer entertainment was had by all, especially the children. Our parents would have friends over with their kids and socialize while watching the children swim and scamper around like a bunch of little hooligans run amok.

The parents would visit and drink their beer and sometimes barbeque. So many summer days and nights would pass in the backyard and at the pool; I believe it was a magical time and place for all of us. I'm also sure many hopes for the future were pinned on it as well. I also know that many of those hopes and dreams would never come to pass, which, in my mind, would be nearly as great a tragedy as the fire that crushed those very hopes and dreams.

There was also a large field across the street where the old grade school had once stood. We would romp and play there or watch the traveling evangelists set up tents when they brought their enthusiastic services to the town.

Mom would always offer her help and visit them before the services commenced. I really can't say how my brothers felt about living there, but I'm hoping, and really do believe, their memories are as great as mine. If they only have one special memory, I hope this is the one they can keep close to their hearts. They don't really talk about it much, but I can get them going sometimes when we reminisce.

In fact, in talking to my brother Chris concerning the book, he believes I need to write what I remember, not what they remember. The idea has great merit, and I will, for the most part, but I can't do that completely.

Some things can be left to whimsy and memory, but some things are far too serious to just go willy-nilly and write what might not be as correct as possible. Although I probably won't go to some of the best sources for my memoirs as I could because I don't want to dredge up old wounds and memories of things that shouldn't have happened yet did. However, nobody will ever remember the exact same things the same way from a time so long ago, now, are they?

The Town

My family and I lived in a small town in central Kansas when I was a young boy. Solomon is a town of about one square mile, one mile long, by about one mile wide. Perfectly 'square,' if you know what I mean. It's located off of I-70 and situated about seven miles west of Abilene. It was a small, seemingly tight-knit, yet contrasting community.

There were few businesses there then, with the School being the largest employer when I lived there. Today, Solomon Corp is the largest employer, which employs maybe 50 or 60 people, if I were to guess. Since Solomon really can be considered a bedroom community, most residents work either in Abilene or Salina or are farmers.

Although Solomon isn't of much importance, historic Abilene had been a famous old Western cattle town where Wild Bill Hickok was a Marshall sometime in the late 1800s. Abilene was also the childhood home of President Dwight D. Eisenhower and is where his museum and library are located and where he and his family are buried.

On the other hand, Solomon had been nothing more than a sleepy little community with around a thousand residents. This figure, of course, didn't include the farmers and other rural families whose children attended our schools.

As teenagers, many of us would go to Abilene on Friday and Saturday nights to cruise up and down Buckeye—the main drag in town. We would either cruise until well past midnight or would get shooed off the streets by the cops because it was after curfew, and usually, it was always the latter of the two.

When we wanted to talk with other 'cruisers,' we would stop at the usual turning places, which was 'the Rock' located near midtown and was south on Buckeye, or the Duckwall-Alco store at the north end of town on Buckeye as well. We had a wonderful time, especially since my best friend, Bob, always had the hottest car in town, whether it was his 66 Chevy Chevelle Super Sport or his 67 Pontiac GTO. Both were hot, sporty, and fast, so we always had fun cruising.

As I look back through my life in Solomon, I can say one thing stands out so obviously in that everyone knew everyone … unless, of course, you were new in town, in which case, it didn't take long before the town's folk came to either know you, or to know about you. The latter usually wasn't a good thing because that meant you had a reputation that might have been frowned upon in our fair little community. However, in Solomon's defense, most people liked almost everyone, regardless of one's character, background, or socioeconomic status, and those that weren't cared for were tolerated.

Solomon was a simple and mostly ordinary little rural community where if you blinked just before entering, you were certain to see it only in your rear-view mirror just as you were leaving. And when I call it a sleepy little town, I'm truly saying that the streets tended to roll up around dark-thirty, regardless of the season.

The only people who could be found after this were the children who dared sneak out at night or the adults who went to the town's bars to socialize. There was, of course, the Sunday exception; they would roll up a little earlier at around dark— rather than dark-thirty.

Yes, there was the occasional event, such as a concert in the park on a warm summer night or when the Boy Scouts had a weekend gathering where area troops would come to camp and have contests to win their medals. This, of course, was to show off their scouting prowess and to have fun as well, I'm sure.

School events, especially sporting events, were another form of community bonding and tradition for the town's citizens, whether Football, Basketball, or Track. I have to believe that if it weren't for these recreational past times, Solomon would not exist today but rather would have died a slow, painful death.

Luckily, Solomon did have a large enough student base to maintain a grade school, Junior High, and High school, which supported many of these functions. The schools were a source of pride then, as I'm sure they are today. And although I stated Solomon was an ordinary town, I would be willing to bet that Solomon's school system is still well above average at giving students a decent education and a sense of pride.

In fact, as an example of its progressiveness, even when I was in school, way back when, around 1978, Solomon was probably the first school in the history of Kansas schools to allow a girl to play on the football team. Her name was Mary Pat Shirack, and she was a little tom-boyish, but she was as sweet a person as anyone would ever want to know. She wasn't the best, of course, but I think she made it through the whole season and gave it the 'ole Gorilla try; the Gorilla was our school mascot, which was unique in its own right.

She just wasn't as physical as she needed to be to keep up, but she had spunk and spirit, which meant a lot. I believe she probably did it just to prove a point, and the next year, she didn't try out for the team.

Along with Mary Pat, Bob, my best friend, and I were also breaking new ground at Solomon High. It was about the same time Mary Pat was playing football. Bob and I had decided to take Home Economics. Now we all know, back then, this was traditionally a girl's class.

I was initially reluctant, and it took some persuading from Bob, but I finally agreed and needless to say, it was quite interesting—especially the fashion show, which I never went to. Nobody ever gave it a second thought or teased us about it. It wasn't long after that other guys took the cue and started enrolling—it wasn't like they were signing up in droves, but a few did.

The Union 76 Truck Stop and Travel Store were built at the interchange of I-70 and county road 221 when I was about 13 or 14. The business was open twenty-four-seven and had many amenities, which included a travel store and a full-service restaurant; we were not used to such amenities, so it was very exciting when it finally opened. It was a quiet gathering spot for the younger crowd but peaked in the late seventies and early eighties.

One of the few things I respected about the business was that it gave us high schoolers a place to work when we wanted money and a place to hang out when we didn't or we were just bored.

Eventually, though, it would fade into nothingness to become a mere memory of a time gone by. The building was eventually converted into a lifeless, lonely old trucking equipment dealership named Chuck Henry Sales, which I believe is still there today, and probably will be for the unforeseeable future.

Solomon had what I would describe as three 'classes' of people: first, there were those who seemed privileged. They lived on the hill many of us called snob knob. This, of course, was located on the 'right' side of the tracks and was pretty much anyone who lived within four or five blocks from the schools.

Then there were those who lived on the 'wrong' side of the tracks; this area was affectionately known as 'cow shit flats' and included the town center and everything south of the tracks.

Finally, the general populace lived on both sides of the tracks but lived modestly. So, Solomon comprised people from various socioeconomic classes but not the extremes. Most everyone got along well enough because even the 'haves' weren't truly wealthy, and the 'have-nots' weren't truly poor; everyone just lived their own lives.

The town had two small full-service gas stations, one owned by Bob Meagher and the other by Roger McKenna. Both were little two-pump stations with two bays where they worked on cars. At McKenna's station, my oldest brother, Chris, nearly had his throat ripped out by the owner's German Sheppard. It was only by a stroke of luck that the dog just missed his jugular vein. He survived, and the scars from the bites are hardly noticeable today.

We had two modest grocery stores; The Hi-Way Market, which sat on old US 40, which ran through the middle of town. This market is still open today, and when I was a kid, it was the place to buy meat. I can't remember who owned it then, but it's been Bush's Market for almost as long as I've known.

The other store was Sankey's Market. Today, Sankey's Market would never be allowed to stay in business because of the many disgusting health violations they would undoubtedly receive. Fortunately, they closed many years ago when people stopped buying there. Whenever I would go there, for whatever reason, it would remind me of something right out of the late 1800s or early 1900s. It was really a blast from the past, but by the time I was in high school, they were only selling non-perishable items.

I recall getting a box of some sort of cake mix for LaDonna Stoltz—LaDonna was one of the ladies I made money babysitting for in town. When she opened the box and poured it into the bowl, it was teaming with mealy worms. I about gagged and swore to never buy anything from there again.

A few years later, they closed down and moved. I believe they sold all their land, including the store and the lot behind it, where they lived in a trailer home. A few years later, the building was demolished, and the land was leveled to make a small corner park.

Three churches were scattered throughout the town: a Catholic church, a Presbyterian church, and a Methodist church. Many Solomonites attended one of the churches, at least on occasion. As if to partner with the three churches, there were three beer joints. All of which were located in the downtown area: Lonnie's Tavern, Velma's Tavern, and the Depot Café.

In retrospect, there were a lot of beer joints for such a small town. All the bars were within a block or two of one another ... I wonder what this said about the townspeople? All these bars changed hands at least a few times over the years. There is only one bar today, and I don't recall its name, but it's only open on the weekends anyway.

Oversimplification is truly an understatement about the town I've just described, but it is certainly a humbling description of the town I remember as a young child. The old High school has been torn down, and a new one erected in its place. The grade school and Junior High remained, with the new High School built between the two. The campus today actually looks much more like a learning center than it did before, which is always good.

Although Solomon has had its good and bad, I would say today, as when I was young, it is still a decent place to raise a family and kids. Also, over time, things always change, as do we all. People change and move on, and new people move in to take their place. And although it is not the same town I knew growing up, it is still good old Solomon in my mind every time I visit.

Chapter 1

An Experiment Gone Wrong—Really Wrong

When I was a child growing up in the heartland, we could probably be considered a typical Midwest family. There was Mom and Dad and us four boys, but we didn't have a family pet then, so I guess we weren't the 'perfect' model of the Midwestern family. I can only recall one other thing that would have made it perfect for me ... a sister; there were no girls, and I had always wanted a sister.

Without any girls, especially older ones, to help, it would have been hard for Mom to care for four rambunctious boys by herself, and how difficult for her it must have been. Dad was very little help, especially since he was always gone, stationed away or out on harvest. I couldn't imagine being a full-time working mother of four boys, all about three years apart between the ages of six and fifteen, and even if I could, I wouldn't want to.

To her credit, and in her sometimes less-than-exemplary manner, she managed to see us through into adulthood; none of us are thieves, rapists, or murderers ... at least that I'm aware of anyway. So, I guess she did okay, although that's not to say we've ever been perfect angels either because we sure as hell aren't, but who really is anyway.

As I described earlier, our home wasn't upscale but was still nice, if not modest. It was a solid, well-built home that could have been quite nice in time. Mom and Dad bought it because it was structurally sound and had lots of room for our growing family. They planned to update the main level and turn the attic into two new bedrooms for Chris and Tom. This, of course, wasn't to be completely realized as unexpected things occurred that put the kibosh on their plans.

The house's interior was designed in a circular fashion, with all the rooms situated on the exterior walls, with the stairwell to the attic surrounded by the interior walls, which served as the center of the home.

I remember you could go through the door at one end of the kitchen and walk into the family room, where the door to the attic was to the left. Walk out of the family room through a short hall with a bedroom off to the right, then into the living room. Hanging a left in the living room would take you through a big set of double doors into Mom and Dad's bedroom. Hanging another left would send you into a hall with the bathroom on the right and the hot water heater in the corner next to the hamper at the end just before you entered back into the other end of the kitchen.

Since the interior of the home was built in this roundabout fashion, and if all the doors were open, you could run circles through the house all day long; in fact, I ended up doing that very thing one sunny Saturday morning ... but believe me, it wasn't for the sheer pleasure of doing so.

The incident that caused this episode was due to my own mischief, which was worthy of getting the belt, and because of Mom's perceived severity of the action, she totally flipped out, and let me tell you, this day ended up sucking worse than all the previous days of my life that sucked put together.

It was a normal Saturday morning, just like any other, except that Bob and I had hatched a plan to do something bad—

very, very bad—from a mom's point of view, anyway. It wasn't evil or anything like that, and to us youngsters, we considered it more of an experiment, something that needed to be explored. After all, most grownups did it, so we never thought it could be such a bad thing.

I was probably eight or nine, and Bob was a year older; we were both in the third grade. Bob was a year older than everyone in our class because he was held back in kindergarten or first grade. Bob and I both got into a lot of trouble growing up, but nothing really too serious—just ordinary stuff that boys do.

Apparently, my only fault for always getting into trouble was that, for whatever reason, I just got on people's nerves; my mom used to tell me that when I was a young kid, I could empty a room just by walking into it. I eventually grew out of it, which would have probably been just when I entered high school.

But the inverse was true of Bob. He became a little more rambunctious the older he got, but eventually, we both changed our ways, and we realized that trouble was something we didn't need, and we both became fairly decent guys, more or less—or as far as anyone knew, anyway.

But on this fateful morning, we were certainly up to no good. It had been my job to acquire our experiment's 'test subject,' as Bob had already secured the means to light it. This was very tricky as I had to get it from Mom, and Mom was no fool. So, as I initiated our plan, Bob lay in wait in the bushes while I obtained the object of our desire.

The lilac bushes behind the house and next to the alley were to provide the cover for our rendezvous. They were very large bushes at about six or seven feet high and quite deep, so there was plenty of room for two small kids to hide while running our experiment.

I tried to walk nonchalantly up to Mom as I began my acquisition of the test subject but was very nervous—I was never a good liar. I began explaining how Bob's mom asked me to come and borrow a cigarette for her. I must have looked like a complete amateur because I remember her looking at me very oddly and asking, "What the hell are you talking about, bird?" She then asked, "When were you down at Bob's?" I told her I had just come from there. Then explained how Dee had asked me just before I left.

This apparently didn't go over too well with Mom because she was hesitant as if wanting to question me further but unsure of the questions to ask. So rather than query any further, she forked it over without much reluctance. I then headed out the door to meet Bob in the bushes; little did I know she was watching me as I left the house.

I can only imagine what she was thinking as she tracked me across the back yard watching me go into the alley and head toward our hiding place. But since she was, in fact, watching, I'm sure she saw the bushes move as I ducked into them. I now realize that, although I walked behind them, I never made it past them … but I didn't think about the possibility that she might have been watching, either.

But being a mother who knows or senses things and me a bumbling stooge, all she had to do was to wait a few moments until we lit the cigarette. She went out the front door because if she were going to catch us, that's how she would've done it, but we two geniuses were watching the back door. She then headed stealthily around the side yard to the back of the house, and as she moved in for the kill—and that's exactly what she did—she took us completely by surprise.

She grabbed me by the arm before I knew what hit me, snatched the cigarette from my hand, and yanked me from the bushes. She growled at Bob in a wild and unseemly manner, telling him he needed to head down the road and get his little ass home.

He shot out of the bushes like a rocket on steroids and didn't look back as he high-tailed it home. I don't think Mom ever told

Dee about it, but if she did, Dee never did anything about it because Bob would have told me. He never said anything about getting into trouble for it afterward, and I was too ashamed of what happened to me to tell him. So, the conversation never came up.

At this age, I was, of course, smaller than Mom in stature, but not much. She stood about five-one and weighed every bit of a hundred pounds, whereas I stood about four and a half feet or so and weighed maybe 70 pounds. She was a fast and powerful woman for her size, and she knew she had to dominate to keep us boys in line. So, although I wasn't too much smaller, she still could manhandle me without much effort.

She was used to playing and fighting with boys because she had been a tomboy growing up, so it came naturally to her. She also showed very little pity when she knew what she had to do needed to be done and knew it wouldn't be easy. This was how she kept control of us—she put the fear of God in us to make sure there was no sass or running amok, and for the most part, it worked to her advantage and fairly well, I might add.

After yanking me out of the bushes, she literally dragged me into the house, all the while screaming and yelling at me for doing the most stupid thing she thought I could ever do, although I only got about one puff before she came barging into our hide-out.

I frantically began apologizing all over myself but to no avail. She pushed me down into a chair at the kitchen table, immediately whipped out a pack of cigarettes, and lit one up. She told me if I wanted to smoke, she would be happy to show me just exactly what it was like to smoke. I sat there puffing my way through about six or seven cigarettes and her lighting the next as I finished each one ... and these were non-filtered cigarettes to boot.

I wasn't allowed to casually smoke either; oh, no, I had to do it in rapid succession, one puff after the other, one cigarette after another. However, I never really inhaled, but I got enough from each puff that by the sixth or seventh cigarette, I was becoming very green around the gills, and this is when it happened.

She yanked me up from the chair and slapped me hard on my ass. She directed me toward the door to the family room and screamed, "Start running, boy!" in a bellow I'd never heard before or wanted to hear again, but on many occasions would anyway.

I took off at a clip. She was in close pursuit and slapping my butt each time I began to slow down or wanted to stop. With each smack, she shouted, "Run!"

After about what seemed like a million laps, I became ill and had to stop to wrench my guts out all over the floor.

She let me finish heaving and hauled me into the bathroom to clean me up. She wasn't through yelling at me, though. She told me in no uncertain terms that there are two things in this world she can't abide: one is a liar, and the other is a thief, and in essence I was, at once, both of those things—by lying to her to get something I wanted, I was in essence, stealing from her.

After she told me this, I understood that I screwed up badly. And on a side note … her 'lesson' eventually settled into my brain and took hold quite nicely. At a formative point in time in my life, I realized I hated both stealing and lying, and from then on to this very day, I don't think I've ever stolen anything on purpose. And as for lying … well, let's just say there's a very subtle and fine line between what is and isn't lying.

I recall one time when I was in my twenties and was coming home from work on the interstate. I was dating my new girlfriend, Jill, who, by the way, was a knock-out. I was filling up in Salina before heading to Solomon, about fifteen miles away.

I was in my own little world thinking about her, just happy as a lark. I finished filling up, got into my car, and daydreamed all the way to the Solomon exit when I realized, "Shit, I forgot to fill up." I immediately looked behind, hoping there were no cops after me.

I was so worried someone saw me and that I was in trouble that I turned around at the Solomon Exit and headed right back to the gas station I had driven off from and paid while apologizing a bazillion times. So, you see, guys, this is how that shit works; it's the fear of God, my friend, the fear of God.

Anyway, Mom cleaned up the floor where I had just heaved, then told me to go to my bedroom and that she would talk to me again later, which she did, but it was only to ask how I was doing and if I wanted some supper.

In retrospect, she had punished me to the fullest extent without doing real and lasting physical harm, but putting the fear of God in me to control the actions of a child doing something that might cause irreparable harm. Had it worked? Yes, at the time, it did. Did it work forever? Not so much, as I've smoked for about 30 years now.

What it really taught me was that you don't mess with the bull if you don't want the horn. However, the real kicker was that Bob and I hadn't been as smart as we thought we were, as it never occurred to us that Mom knew Dee Houser didn't smoke, and that's how we were really caught red-handed—ironic, huh?

By today's standards, this would be considered child abuse. Back then, however, it was more acceptable, but not something you advertised, and it was common practice to use almost any form of punishment, just short of serious or lasting physical abuse, to correct a child's bad behavior. And usually, the punishment fit the crime.

Looking back today, it was really comical as I watch her chasing me around the house that day in my mind, and what she did may seem bizarre by today's standards, but it is another memory I will keep, and believe it or not, cherish for the rest of my life.

Chapter 2

Burnin' Down the House

After the smoking fiasco, nothing else of importance occurred for the rest of the summer other than probably the most devastating thing to happen to my family, but not to me.

Albert was six years old; I was nine, Tom was twelve, and Chris was fifteen when the fire occurred. Chris had been old enough to babysit the rest of us for the past few years whenever Mom needed a sitter. Regrettably, on this night, one of my most enduring memories was of what occurred when he was doing just this—babysitting us boys. Neither he nor anyone else in our lives could have ever imagined in our wildest nightmares that this could ever happen.

It was a warm summer evening, late one Friday or Saturday sometime in 1972. I remember because Dad was still away on harvest, and we kids hadn't gone back to school yet. Mom had decided to go out dancing earlier in the evening. She never told me she was going out, but she had, of course, told Chris and maybe Tom.

I, however, knew she was going out because she was all dressed up with her makeup on and her hair done up just right, and whenever she got gussied up, you knew she was going drinking and dancing in Salina. Had she only been going to the bar downtown, she would have made herself up, but not to the extent she had that night, and she wouldn't have called a friend to take her there, either.

Although Mom would surely be drinking that night, she was always responsible in that when she did drink, she would use a designated driver; as far as I know, Mom never had a DUI— this wasn't always the case, as far as drinking and driving went anyway.

I remember Dad eventually got to the point that when we needed another car, he would simply buy one that was what he called 'pre-dented' to save Mom the trouble of denting it herself; of course, it was only a joke, but in reality, it was probably closer to the truth. Regardless, Mom knew if she was drinking, she needed a driver, and that was why Wayne Duncan showed up at the door that night.

As I recall, Wayne, a family friend, was a real hick of a guy and not much of a party animal: very conservative, quiet, low-key, and completely harmless. He had the occasional beer but was never a real drinker. It was because of these traits I believe Mom felt safe asking him to chaperone her whenever she wanted to go to town.

Mom and Dad loved to dance, and Mom had become accustomed to doing so even when Dad was away. Dad, of course, knew and apparently was just fine with the arrangement. I'm also fairly certain she never cheated on Dad, although sometimes I wondered why they ever stayed together … but that's a story for another chapter. Mom was a drinker then, but she hadn't yet turned into the alcoholic she was to become one day.

After Mom and Wayne left, us boys fiddle-dinked around for a while, and when it was time for bed, Chris sent me and

Albert to our room while he and Tom stayed up to watch TV. Eventually, they fell asleep in the living room. Chris and Tom usually slept upstairs in the attic but hadn't that night, as they were busy watching TV.

I don't know if this was the reason for sure, but I'm truly glad they didn't sleep up there on that night. I can only thank God that at least one of the fates smiled upon us on this particular night. With them in the living room and me and Albert in our bedroom, which was just across the room at the end of the little hall, we were all sound asleep when the fiasco quietly began.

Sometime later in the night, Chris was awakened by the smell of smoke. He instantly scrambled to his feet to see where it was coming from. He didn't have to look too far or too long as the smoke was gently billowing from the hall outside Mom and Dad's bedroom. It wasn't very thick, but enough so that he began coughing, which was loud enough to stir Tom but not quite awaken him.

Chris began putting out what had been a small fire once he discovered it was coming from near the clothes hamper at the end of the hall. Apparently, some clothes were thrown at, but not into, the hamper, which happened to be next to the gas water heater. For some damn reason, there wasn't a guard over the pilot light, leaving it open to the surroundings. Why there wasn't a cover on it, who knows, but as such, a piece of clothing found its way inside, or at least close enough to catch fire.

Chris was nearly finished snuffing out the fire when Tom finally awakened to realize smoke was everywhere. He hollered for Chris, immediately ran to where he was, and asked what was happening. Chris explained the situation in short order and told him to open all the windows while he finished getting things under control. Chris knew they needed to get the stench of smoke out of the house before Mom got home because the smell was now beginning to saturate everything inside.

I'm fairly certain Chris felt if Mom came home to the smell of smoke throughout the house, she would have been seriously pissed. And since he was in charge, he would have been in trouble. I'm also sure she wouldn't have blamed him but would have thanked God nothing worse had happened.

I don't think Chris was thinking this way, though; he was probably more worried about staying out of trouble than thinking she would thank him for keeping the house from burning down and possibly killing us boys.

Once Tom and Chris were satisfied that the situation was under control, they went back to the living room to watch TV and, again, fell asleep. Albert and I were none the wiser and slept through the whole commotion as if it had never happened. However, within the hour, it would seem all hell was breaking loose and that the end of the world was upon us, standing only just outside on the front doorstep, waiting to slip inside and steal everything away that was dear to us.

Within an instant, it did just that, and afterward, without so much as a thank you or a kiss goodbye, we were left standing there alone and terrified with only the clothes on our backs, as if we were of no consequence whatsoever.

Chris had thought he doused the flame. He never realized that it might have gotten inside the hollow area of the wall where it would hide like a rabid dragon, waiting silently to ambush its unsuspecting victims. Slowly, the fire would work its way up through the wall and into the attic. Once there, it had begun spreading violently enough so that the roar of the crackling fire would awaken them once more.

Again, they desperately began searching the house for signs of the fire's presence, hearing it but not seeing it; the noise seemed to be coming from everywhere and getting louder as the moments ticked by. Tom eventually found smoke coming through the top and sides of the attic's stairwell door in the family room and screaming at the top of his lungs, he yelled to Chris that he found it.

Chris came running to where Tom stood just before the door. They both stared at it as if knowing there was some hideous monster behind it, waiting to lunge at them if they opened it. But Tom, in an act of desperation from the fear they were feeling and the need to know exactly how bad things were, threw open the door with a flurry. As it flew open, the smoke and flames came billowing down through the stairwell and out at them through the opening.

The fire raged at them with a roaring fury. It slammed Tom back into Chris with a blast of heat and flames. At that moment, they knew that all the dread they had hoped against had materialized into a true-life horror. One hundred percent genuine terror instantly snatched them into its grip, and all at once, they took off shrieking and screaming, high tailing it to awaken Albert and me and get us all outside to safety.

They came rushing into our room, just down the hall, blaring at the top of their lungs, "FIRE, FIRE!" Their voices resonated over our heads like the piercing sounds of two screaming mee-mies. They were shaking us frantically while pulling us from our beds and yelling, "GET UP! GET UP!"

We scrambled from our beds, and although we were a little dazed and confused, Albert and I were up and at 'em within seconds. My heart was racing a thousand miles a minute, not from the fire but from Tom and Chris scaring the crap right out of me. Albert was completely confused and jumping up and down on the bed, shrieking at the top of his lungs.

No sooner than we hit the floor did I begin screaming as wildly as Albert. For a moment, it was as if everything was becoming blurry. I became woozy and lightheaded. However, we collected our wits within seconds and began performing like pros. As we ran out the bedroom door, we must have looked like a bunch of wild Jack rabbits exploding from their wallow when something stepped too close.

With nothing on but our skivvies, Albert and I were in high gear and shot from the room like two cannonballs. Once in the living room, we dashed out the front door with Chris in hot pursuit. Tom, however, wasn't following as we ran onto the front porch. Worried, Chris told us to keep running, then ripped around to head back to see what happened to Tom.

He found Tom had detoured into Mom and Dad's bedroom to collect some clothes since we were all nearly nude. I could hear them yelling at each other, but within a minute or so, Chris shot back onto the porch and down to where Albert and I were waiting.

Tom had darted into Mom and Dad's bedroom, where a pile of clean clothes lay on the bed waiting to be folded. He was nervously picking through them when Chris found him. Screaming, Chris yelled at him to just grab as much as he could and throw them out the window.

Unsure that he had grabbed enough the first time, he took another armful and flew out the window with them, landing on the pile of clothes he already threw out. He wasn't more than twenty seconds behind Chris when he landed on the porch. We all then ran over, grabbed the clothes, and headed lickety-split to the safety of the street.

Fortunately, they had previously opened all the windows, which kept the smoke from pervading so much that we couldn't breathe or see what we were doing during our escape. But it was getting bad, and within minutes, it began consuming the inside of the home like a vile and ravenous dragon, belching fire and smoke after devouring anything that got in its way.

We were working on instinct and pure adrenaline with only survival on our minds. But, in real-time, and because it all happened so fast, I don't think we had time to be frightened, even after we were safe and could begin processing exactly what was going down. The entire scene lasted only minutes, but it appeared so dreamlike and bizarre, as if time and space were moving in some deliriously slow, undulating motion.

When Chris was sure we were all safe, he shot off like a rocket, jetting down the block to the park where a payphone was located on the corner. He called the operator, which was free back then, who alerted the city's volunteer fire department to the situation; Solomon was such an easygoing and quiet town, even on the weekends, so it doesn't surprise me now that by the time they arrived, most of the home was engulfed by fire and beyond saving—although they tried.

Before their arrival, we could only stare at the oppressive flames shooting up into a silent void of black nothingness. They seemed to go on forever, up into the dark night sky, as if the filthy beast was lapping from a murky, endless pool of water, trying to quench its insatiable thirst after hungrily devouring its latest victim.

By now, people from around the neighborhood began congregating out in the street in front of the house. They were running around hollering for us kids. We were all in the same general vicinity but weren't right beside one another. Eventually, they rounded us all up, ensuring we were all there and alright. Then they began hastily urging us for information, wanting to know what happened, where everyone was, and whether we were okay.

I remember one person kept nervously asking Chris over and over again if our parents were home or if anyone else was in the house. Still a bit dazed, Chris screamed that we were the only ones at home and told her to leave him alone. Just then, as if timing were everything, Mom and Wayne came flying up, a feat unto itself as Wayne usually drove like a turtle on downers.

Mom flew out of the car before Wayne had even stopped. She didn't miss a lick and began running toward the house. She was pushing people out of her way, screaming hysterically, and howling for her babies. But two people grabbed and held her back before she got too close to the fire or even located any of us. She kept flailing around, wildly pleading, "Where're my babies! Oh God, where are my babies!"

If allowed, I have to think that she would have run dead into the fire believing she could save the boys she thought she had lost. But the fire was so hot, even as they sprayed water to quench the flames, a person couldn't have gotten within fifty feet of it. But Mom being Mom, and knowing what she is capable of, would have certainly tried had she not been stopped. After being constrained, and with perfect grace, she surrendered to her fears and fainted in their arms. Once she went limp, they laid her down on the street.

An interesting side note here was when I was discussing this with Tom, one thing he remembered very well about that night was that when Mom passed out, one of the firemen became pissed because he couldn't move his hose. He screamed at the men who laid her down to get her the hell off his hose.

Tom said he was so pissed, and even in its retelling, I could see the anger well up in his eyes and wash over his face. These so-called 'volunteer' firemen were late getting to the house, to begin with, and by the time they were getting the fire under control, the house was already well past saving. I think the bastard could have shown a little respect and compassion, and I would also say he can thank his lucky stars we didn't recognize him that night because, as our family goes, we usually don't tend to forget stuff like that.

After moving to a more open, less chaotic spot, the men laid her back down. A couple of women saw what happened, came over, and knelt beside her. They gently slapped her face saying, "Joyce ... Joyce, honey, wake up ... wake up," which they kept doing until she finally came to a few minutes later.

As these ladies were rousing her, I became more aware of and focused on the scene around me. I began noticing the people running all about the place while shouting directions to whoever would listen, appearing as if they had done this very thing regularly. I guess when people are faced with the challenges of a calamity, they can cope pretty well, at least enough to get things done.

My mind finally caught up with time, and I was taking in the whole situation earnestly. I noticed the light from the flames and how they cast an eerie glow over my mother's seemingly lifeless face as she lay on the ground. Then my eyes shifted to the pandemonium around us. Again, it was very surreal, and the flickering light from the flame appeared to give the shadows their own life.

They seemed to transform into little demons, dancing and darting in and out of the fire's unnatural radiance. At this time, I started becoming scared … really scared, but I bit it back and somehow managed to keep it mostly together. I had no idea how any of my brothers were doing mentally or emotionally, but I'm sure they were feeling just what I was at the time.

Mom was now coming to, so some man gathered us kids and brought us over to show her we were okay, which somewhat calmed her. She began to sob uncontrollably and hugged us like little rag dolls. After taking a few moments to ensure we were okay and it wasn't a dream, she turned her attention to the fire and chaos in front of us.

I can recall the devastation on her face and the reflection of the flames in her eyes as the fire continued to engulf the house. Looking back, I can so clearly see the life and future she had so carefully planned drain from her eyes with every tear she shed as she stood there completely and utterly helpless. It was at this moment I believe my mom's life began its long, slow spiral into a life that none of us would wish upon ourselves or upon anyone for that matter.

As God as my witness, I could never imagine in a million years the horror that was torturing her mind and soul just as she was pulling up to the fire, that her four children were burned alive in the home that was now completely destroyed. There really is no way of knowing to what extent the damage from that type of mental anguish could inflict or would cause, or that she would have to bear the rest of her life.

I only know that her family had to bare much of her pain too, and to some degree, that would harm us children far more than the fire had. It's only a shame that it wasn't until the last few years of her life that I had truly come to know my mother as I wish I could have all my life. And I wish my brothers had also come to know her as I did.

As for my dad, I'm not sure when he finally learned of the fire, but I'm sure when he did, it didn't impact him in the same manner or to the extent it did Mom. This was because he never felt the overwhelming dread of thinking you've lost your children in such a dreadful manner. I believe his life was profoundly changed, though, as this was also his dream. And also, because his life was so inextricably tied to Mom's and what she would go through later, he would have to go through as well.

I believe that Mom blamed herself for the tragedy that night, not only from her absence but the circumstances under which she was absent, and maybe Dad, to some extent, blamed her as well. Something I don't think either of them, or we kids, ever realized, but upon reexamination of the whole episode, I believe I do. Even if she had been there that night, the fire would still have happened because whether it was her or Chris putting out the small fire, it still would have continued as it did.

Tom and Chris thought the fire was out, and it wasn't; therefore, she would have thought the same way. The real difference would have been that Tom and Chris would probably have been sleeping upstairs because Mom would have put them to bed. Had this occurred, I'm sure it would have been a far worse tragedy. So, in essence, I suppose, Mom probably saved Tom and Chris, as well as Albert and me that night. But I'm sure neither she nor anyone else ever realized this as I have.

Any way you cut it, this was when we all began the long, slow journey to becoming the family we are today, which isn't necessarily all bad or bad at all times, but it can certainly be trying sometimes. Yes, there have been good times throughout our lives, but it has certainly been a long and rocky road for all of us—worse for some of us than others.

After the fire, our parents located places for us boys to live until they could settle matters enough to bring us back together. The three older kids stayed with our own friends, and since Albert was so young, he stayed with Mom and Dad at Besses and Dad Luck's. Dad Luck was the father of Mom's oldest and closest friend, Barbara Hale, and Mom's and Barb's families would become life-long friends. Bess was Dad Luck's second wife and not the mother of Barbara, but I believe the grandkids considered her their grandmother, and everyone loved Dad Luck.

Over time, we recovered to some degree, or as well as expected, but life would never be the big, happy family we were before the fire. As Mom and Dad have passed away many years ago, the boys have moved on. As I said, at times, things are good in our lives, and at times, not so much, but we are survivors and will persevere as we always have.

As I write this chapter, I vividly recall hearing Wayne talking to Dad one day about the fire. In a very low and puzzled voice, he said, "George, driving home that night from Salina, we were about two or three miles outside of town, and as soon as Joyce saw the fire's glow, she immediately knew it was your house that was burning. I couldn't drive fast enough for her, and then she just became hysterical out of nowhere. She began hitting me, wanting me to go faster and trying to push down the gas pedal. It was all I could do to keep her away from me." Dad never really responded to Wayne, only giving a little "Humph." After that, I don't recall discussing the fire with anyone in the family until writing this book.

I will always have fond memories of our first true home. The memories of Chris, Tom, Albert, and me making Roger Rip-Rocket oatmeal cookies in the summer; snow ice cream in the winter; and having contests playing tanks on the bed with all these guys I call my brothers. This truly was the only innocent and magical time in my life. And you, the reader, will get to know more about me, my family, and my friends as we go through the chapters of my life, and in the end, I want you to be as comfortable with me as I am with writing my story for you.

Chapter 3

House Hoppin': The Family Past Time

The Little Pink House

The name for this chapter is appropriate, and if things didn't finally come to settle down, it could probably have been named "House Hoppin'; It's A Family Tradition" as we moved five times in about four years after the fire. Although the Old Red Brick House isn't depicted in this chapter, it will be given its due once we move into it later in another chapter.

It was late summer 1972, after the house burned down when Mom and Dad finally decided to stay in Solomon. They had rented a little pink house next to the Carlson funeral home. They had wanted the family back together before school started, knowing we needed stability and continuity.

The home was nice but very pink and small compared to our previous home. This, of course, wasn't to be the home Mom and Dad planned on staying in for any length of time, only long enough to make their next move toward getting completely settled—which seemed like an eternity. Their ultimate goal was to become homeowners again so they could have something to call their own; even a shanty would have been fine with them; as long as it was theirs.

There wasn't much going on with Mom and Dad while living in the pink house or with us kids. However, there was one interesting 'incident' that occurred not long after moving in, and it happened to be a fairly significant ordeal, as my brother, Tom, recalled while we were talking about old times one night.

I also think this incident probably hastened Mom and Dad's desire to move from the house even sooner than they might have otherwise. Although it was serious at the time, it's mostly comical as I recollect it, and it really is a wonderful showcase of Mom's finer attributes as they relate to her interpersonal relations with people who piss her off.

When we were growing up, Mom and Dad had less-than-stellar reputations due to their drinking, which on many occasions would invariably dissolve into arguing and fighting, and most, if not all, the townspeople knew it. So, when we moved in, our next-door neighbor didn't necessarily greet us with open arms.

I'm sure he felt his family was better than ours because of this; therefore, we weren't the type of family he wanted living next door. But you know, in Solomon, it was just like one big neighborhood, so why it bothered him then and not before is anyone's guess.

I suppose to some degree I can sort of maybe understand this reaction, but only to a small degree since Mom and Dad's wild fighting days were mostly behind them once we moved into the home that burned down; although through the years, they would still have a few battles that were real doozies.

They still drank, sometimes to excess, but the arguments were much more subdued and, over the past couple of years, became further and fewer between. But nonetheless, he had us pegged as a bunch of low-life, ne're-do-wells even though this most certainly wasn't the case at that time.

However, this is something I never understood as it concerned us children. We weren't hellions or delinquents and were actually pretty decent kids. Yes, we had made a few mistakes, but nothing to be considered more than childhood rambunctiousness. I suppose it was more concerned with, you know, the sins of the parents.

We weren't neighborly material to him, and he didn't want us within his sphere of existence. Still, in our defense, we were not white trash, and I think this was what he was alluding to when he and Mom got into it one day when she went next door to pay them a visit.

They were the Rock family, and the father, Jerry, was a real piece of work. Unfortunately for him, because of a stupid comment he made and the subsequent row between him and Mom, it would become his Day of Judgment and reckoning as far as she was concerned.

He knew her reputation, as did everyone in town. Sober or drinking, she could be belligerent and brash when you pissed her off, and the more you pissed her off, the louder and more unbearable she became.

I have no idea to this day what he could possibly have been thinking or what in the world could ever have possessed the man to make such a thoughtless, hateful, and completely ill-conceived remark as he had that day—other than his own stupidity.

It was a Saturday morning, and we kids had been watching cartoons on the television when Mom informed us she was going next door to meet with the Rocks. She already knew him because he was the butcher at the Hi-way Market. I guess she thought it was still a good idea to pay them a visit as they were our new neighbors, and I don't think Mom had really ever talked much with his wife, whose name escapes me.

So, to her surprise, she had no suspicion that he harbored any contempt for her or her family. He never acted in any manner other than to be friendly whenever she ordered meat from him. Consequently, she was thoroughly blindsided by his reaction to our family moving in next door.

Jerry had been the one to answer the door when she knocked. Of course, being a tomboy and from the South, she was not shy, but she always tried to be charming, polite, and neighborly. Well, folks, this was not going to be one of those days when her southern 'charm' would be on display, and let me tell you, when he said what he said, she instantly turned on him and was hell-bent for leather.

She made this poor man look like a complete idiot and utter fool, or at least it did to us kids. Luckily for us, the window behind the television was open and afforded a bird's eye view of Jerry's front porch, maybe 25 feet away. The scene that transpired when Jerry stepped outside and closed the door behind him was downright terrifying and awesome at the same time.

He must have been quite blunt in his remarks because they were quarreling within a minute or two. When we heard the argument begin, we jumped up from the floor and darted over to shut off the television. Tom shushed us and told us to listen so we could hear what they were arguing about, and I can certainly tell you we got one hell of an earful.

They were all up in arms, yelling back and forth with fingers pointing in every which direction, but mostly at one another. She called him a few choice words and abruptly turned around to head down the stairs. As she did, Jerry, in a loud voice, said, "If the McMillans are moving in, then the Rocks are moving the fuck out!"

Oh, how this was a big mistake; to say something vulgar like that to Mom was an incredibly serious no-no in her book. You don't ever speak to her in this manner and not expect some serious retribution. To say cuss words like that to her, especially about her family and in public … hmmm, my, my, shit was about to hit the fan, my friend, and that's exactly what went down on that fine, sunny Saturday morning.

She immediately did an about-face and said with complete indignation, "Well then, you better start packing your bags, you son of a bitch, 'cause the McMillans are movin' in!"

We could see he was trying to get a word in edgewise, but she would interrupt before he got the chance. She finally finished what she started and said, "Whether you like it or not, you lousy, no good-for-nothing piece of shit!"

"WOW!" was the only thing we kids could say as we stared at one another in total shock and awe. I never heard Mom use those words except when fighting with Dad, so for him to say those words to her in public was only asking for exactly what he got.

Jerry just stood there shell-shocked. For a moment, he was speechless, but what the hell did he expect; "Thank you, Mr. Rock," "Sorry for the intrusion, Mr. Rock." I don't think so. I'm sure he had expected her to reply angrily but not so loudly and graphically.

Dumbfound and visibly shaken, he quickly turned to go back inside, simply shaking his head. On his way in, though, he muttered something under his breath. We, kids, couldn't hear what he said, but Mom sure did, and again, it absolutely infuriated her. She had just made it back to the steps and began marching up them as Jerry disappeared into the house.

However, before he could slam the door shut, she yelled in the loudest voice I'd ever heard come out of her little five-foot-and-one-inch stature, screaming, "Oh ya, you chicken shit! You're not man enough, but I bet your old lady is, so why don't you send her out, and I'll kick her ass instead!" We could only guess what he might have said, but it seemed pretty obvious.

Our jaws just then hit the floor. I don't think he had realized exactly what Mom could do or say when she was really pissed … hell, at that point, I don't think we really did either. Had he truly wanted to kick her ass, if, in fact, that's what he said, I'll guarantee she would have been more than happy to oblige, fighting him right then and there for God and the whole world to see. She was scrappy in her day, and she never backed down … no matter who you were or who you thought you might be.

Chris immediately shut the window when she began heading down the sidewalk to the house. When she walked inside, we asked what happened, but she wouldn't answer. She was noticeably shaken. Mom never gave anyone any shit unless they asked for it or she felt it was due. But on that one day, Jerry's special day, she sure gave him a bucket full of it and with both barrels a-blazin'. She was not a woman afraid of making sure that anyone within earshot knew what was going on and what she thought about Jerry on that one special day so many years ago.

This is not to say Mom was a bad person at all—or was always like this—it was just her way; she would give you the shirt off her back if you were in need, friend or foe, because she wasn't a petty woman. She was very much a generous woman; you just didn't want to get on her wrong side too often or become too hostile with her at any time.

People who knew her either loved or hated her, but many respected her. Two things she used to tell us kids when we were growing up was one, the bigger they are, the harder they harder they fall, and two, the smaller they are, the further they fly.

We never found out exactly what Jerry said to her that day, but she did tell Dad, of course. When he came home that night, she told him what happened that day as they sat at the kitchen table after supper. They talked about many other things as well, but the one thing I knew they were talking about was that they would begin looking for another place to live.

Mom couldn't stand the man next door now and told Dad it would only worsen if they stayed. In essence, although Jerry had lost the battle, he had won the war. This was, however, only because she knew it would eventually get really ugly, and she didn't want to put us kids through another ordeal, especially since she could avoid it, unlike the tragedy of the fire.

We remained in the pink house for the rest of the school year, and, to Mom's credit, she did a good job of staying away from the Rocks as she instructed us to do as well. As soon as school let out for the summer, though, Mom and Dad found another house, but it wasn't in Solomon. When I was ten years old, we moved to Niles, Kansas.

The Niles House

Niles was a small rural community about seven or eight miles west and a little north of Solomon. It was in the middle of nowhere, Kansas, and as far as I was concerned, it was like living in purgatory. Luckily, we knew all the kids in town because they all went to school in Solomon because Niles was in Solomon's school district. The population was maybe seventy-five people; if I stretch it, maybe a hundred, tops.

A couple of the main differences of living in the country for me was that we had to ride the school bus, which was a definite change that I could've easily done without, and all my friends still lived in Solomon, and I could only see them while at school or the occasional sleep-over. Hell, that summer, I couldn't even go swimming since there wasn't so much as a wading pool in that town, so I was bored out of my gourd the whole summer there.

I hated riding the bus, and I would never wish riding a bus to school on anybody. Again, I believe going to the same school we were used to give us boys a sense of stability and continuity … for what it was worth, but that would be overshadowed by Mom and Dad's arguing, which flared back up again.

I don't recall what happened between them, but they were not getting along. They were arguing and fighting constantly, and it was only getting worse. I feel it probably had to do with the house burning down and the moving and upheaval that was going on in our lives, but it was to continue off and on for most of the rest of their lives.

It would be good sometimes and bad at other times, but it wasn't until the kids were grown up that they slowed it down to a 'respectable' level again, and by the time they were both in their mid-to-late fifties did it pretty much completely stop.

You have to remember that we had lost everything in the world, even the shirts off our backs, literally. The townspeople of Solomon had really been quite generous, which helped Mom and Dad get back on their feet. The loss of our home was an incredible blow to them, and that loss would burn a gaping hole right through their very souls.

The anguish never completely faded away to be forgotten but only suppressed in their memories by time and alcohol. So in the wake of their misery, it would inherently always leave our family in a state of repression, leading to constant conflict.

While in Niles, Mom and Dad finally split up. Mom stayed with her friend Doris in Salina while dad stayed home and cared for us. In retrospect, I believe this was a ruse by Mom, as she would never leave or abandon her children. I think she used it as a ploy to try and blackmail Dad into being more responsive to her, or at least cooperative to the degree that might help alleviate their arguments. But regardless of the reasons, they separated.

She was gone for only a couple weeks or so and had been in contact with Dad the entire time. I'm not sure what they talked about when they were in contact, but I'm fairly certain it wasn't all the best they wished for each other. We constantly asked Dad when Mom was coming home, and he always answered, "Soon." I don't believe he was so sure, though, but it helped soothe us for the moment.

As I said, a couple of weeks or so went by when she finally came home. All of us kids were glad, and I believe Dad was too. The only good I thought came from her absence was that there was peace and quiet for a good while afterward. It did seem to alleviate the frequency and severity of their arguments. Still, over time, the peace was to become only a faded memory. We continued living in Niles for the rest of the school year and ended up back in Solomon the summer of my eleventh year.

The Brick House

I was eleven and entering the sixth grade when we moved into an old two-story, red brick house next to the Solomon Co-op. We had moved only about a block and a half from the pink house where we had previously lived, which was now green. And yes, the Rocks still lived next door.

The distance was far enough to create a buffer zone, but Mom never bought meat from Jerry or shopped at the Hi-way market again. She knew it was better to leave sleeping dogs lie rather than to wake them only to have them bite you in the ass again.

This house, too, wasn't to be the home in which we would set down roots as we still had one more to go through before that happened. It was only another stop-over in the long, difficult journey to the home we called 'The Old Red Brick House.'

This house had a large yard and plenty of room inside and out for playing and growing. However, this was the house where I first met death on a personal level, and it was the only thing that happened while living there that would greatly impact me during my childhood.

We had a family dog, and his name was Brownie. He was maybe two years old when we got him. He was a very gentle, medium-sized mutt weighing maybe forty or so pounds, but he was a full and loved member of our family. Dad was the one who mostly took care of him, so he was probably the most attached to the dog, or so I thought.

One boring and hot summer day, my friend Stan Heitsman and I decided to go fishing. Stan was a couple years older than me. His grandmother, Naomi, and my mom were friends, and they always had drinks together, so Stan and I became friends as kids.

Naomi had taken Stan in as a young child after his parents died in a car accident. Eventually, though, Stan and I grew apart as he began hanging out with kids his own age when he entered high school.

On this day, though, we decided on Blue Sands Lake for our fishing excursion, which was just a large pond. Actually, it was an old sand pit located about three or four miles just west and a little north of town. It was a good place to fish, but probably the furthest away.   The fastest and easiest way to get to the lake on foot was by walking the ditches next to Interstate 70, which ran right next to the lake. So just after lunch, we headed there on foot along with Brownie.

We made it there without much trouble in about an hour or so and, as always, enjoyed ourselves along the way. Being part of our little troupe that day, Brownie was always running ahead, bounding through the bushes and weeds, or staying behind when he found something interesting to sniff.

He was a high-spirited animal and would only lie down after he had exhausted himself through the course of his daily adventures. He also wasn't an inside dog so much and usually slept on the porch, except in the extreme cold of winter or during thunderstorms in the spring and summer.

We fished for most of the afternoon but always threw back anything we caught because we didn't want to lug it back to town. Fishing was another one of the things we did for entertainment growing up as kids during the summers in Kansas; we would usually make our own fun, and it usually kept us out of trouble.

We had been walking along the north side of the highway on our way home, which was the same side the lake was on. However, the Solomon River made it impossible to travel all the way back to town without getting back onto the interstate, so we eventually crossed over when we reached the river.

While crossing the bridge, we decided to go ahead and cross to the other side of the road, where we would eventually need to be anyway. Once on the shoulder, we looked both ways where the coast had been clear; in both directions, the lanes were empty as far as we could see. When we headed across, Brownie suddenly took off back into the ditch to investigate something moving in the grass.

I called for him to get back over to me, but he kept probing and stiffing the grass. I headed back across the road to see if I could grab him by his collar and, if necessary, pull him back across with me. Little did Stan, or I know that a car was speeding toward us by the time this occurred, about a mile or so away. Back in those days, there weren't any speed limits on the highways. So, about the time I crossed the road to where Brownie was sniffing around, he came bounding toward me.

I turned to head back to where Stan was waiting, thinking Brownie would follow. I made it back across the road and again turned to see Brownie sniffing around on the concrete shoulder of the road; he was still on the other side of the highway, though.

Just then, I noticed the car I hadn't seen earlier; it couldn't have been more than twenty or thirty seconds away. I looked at Brownie, and for a moment, I was surprised; I was just standing there. I thought I had time to run across, but by the time I realized what was going on, I didn't know what to do or why I couldn't do it had I known.

I came back to reality in a rush, but it was too late to run across the road. I was afraid to holler for him to come to me and didn't want to tell him to stay, not knowing whether either would send him running across the road in front of the car. In my mind and heart, right then, at that very moment, I knew what would happen. My pulse raced wildly, and I could hear the blood rushing to and through my brain.

All I could do was stand there as if frozen in time. Stan didn't move or say a word as we looked at one another. It was as if we both connected mentally at that moment through our glances and body language. We knew something terrible was about to happen, and sure enough, about the time the car was within one hundred or so feet, Brownie looked up at me and, in a joyful leap, shot across the highway directly in front of the car.

As I remember, it was a dull thud, and there were no yelps or cries of agony. My dog was hurled down the road about fifty or sixty feet, and if he wasn't killed upon the initial impact, he certainly was when the car ran him over, tumbling him all the way from the front to the back of the car only to be shot out the back where he rolled for another ten or twenty feet. I stood there horrified and in shock. I was unable to move a muscle or think a thought. Stan was, though, and he ran over to grab and shake me back to my senses.

Just as the car began to slow down, I snapped to. We ran over to where Brownie was lying in a small pool of blood that began collecting around his mangled body. The car never stopped completely, and as we reached my dog, it sped away.

In thinking about it, it was as if the driver couldn't have cared less or didn't have the time to deal with what they had just done. This would've never happened had they been paying attention to their driving. However, had I not taken him with me, it also would've never happened.

I stood there, over my dog, watching the car move down the road, disappearing to become only a spec in the distance as if it had never been there at all. The most hateful thoughts

I could muster began racing through my mind. I felt as if my heart would explode through my chest at that very moment as I held my breath to keep from screaming and cursing the person who'd just murdered my dog.

The tears didn't just well into my eyes; they came rushing out in a torrent of hate and misery. A lump in my throat made it nearly impossible to breathe or swallow. I was absolutely mortified. Within a few moments, my mind cleared enough to begin collecting myself and my thoughts but only with Stan's help.

I knelt down next to my Brownie, all the while sobbing uncontrollably. Brownie was a mass of tangled legs, bloody, matted hair, and lifeless black pools of darkness where his eyes once sparkled. There was no life in him whatsoever.

His tongue dangled from his mouth as if he were still panting. Blood had poured from his mouth, and the areas where the hair had been scraped from his body had left his tissue as if someone had tried scalping him with a dull butter knife.

As I was kneeling next to him, I went to lift him into my arms, but he was completely limp. I moved him off the road to the shoulder and sat with him in my arms. Stan kept saying how sorry he was, all the while wondering out loud what we were going to do. I had no idea myself, but I just got sick to my stomach and could only cry repeatedly, "Oh God! Oh God! Brownie!"

Once I was somewhat collected, we started carrying him but only made it about a hundred or so feet. We knew we wouldn't be able to get him back to town because he was too big, and it was too far, and I was beginning to get soaked with his blood, and I just couldn't keep the tears from streaming down my cheeks.

We stopped for a minute so I could collect my wits and we could collect our thoughts. We needed to formulate a plan as to what to do about the poor animal. We first agreed that we couldn't bury him because we had no shovel, so that plan wasn't possible. We finally decided there were only two options available, or at least in our minds at the time, but we had to decide which was the best.

The first plan was to leave him on the side of the road and walk back to get someone to take him into town. However, I didn't like this idea because I didn't want him lying there in the open for the flies and all manner of creatures to intrude on his torn and broken body. And I also didn't want anyone to see him in such terrible shape. The other avenue was much less civilized, but at least nothing would ever bother him as he made his way slowly to the sea. We then agreed on this, our second plan.

We turned and walked back to the Solomon River bridge. It was a long hundred feet or so, but not because of Brownie's weight or size, but because I knew what was about to happen was to be something I had to live with and was almost ashamed to do it then.

I have never forgotten, nor will I ever forget, what I did that day, and as I look back upon the things I have done or been forced to do, for the good, bad, or indifference to it all, I felt I was doing the best thing for my dog.

• The tangle of trees, bushes, and vines had made getting to the water's edge virtually impossible, so we walked to the middle of the bridge, where I lay brownie down on the top of the concrete railing and gave out a huge moaning sigh. The river was about twenty or thirty feet below. It was meandering, and the water was flowing along at a snail's pace, I thought.

I looked at Stan, who asked in a muted and distant tone, "Are you sure you want to do this, Bird?" I, of course, didn't and pondered the question for a long moment before, in a quivering, almost inaudible voice, said, "Yes."

At that moment, my heart and soul sank to the bottom of a very deep and dark abyss. For an instant, I thought to myself, "Oh God! Is this what I'm supposed to do? But without answering my own question and with great restraint, I gently pushed my friend over the edge. I began sobbing quietly, knowing I would never see my old friend again, and then, as one might expect, I questioned my actions and thought, *What in the world have I done? Oh God, what have I done?*

Then, as if regretting my actions, I wondered aloud, "Do people really throw their dogs over a bridge?" I didn't know how to answer my own questions, nor did Stan, who stood quietly close by. Looking back, I realize it might not have been the brightest or the right thing to do, but at the time, it was all I felt I could do.

Brownie made a gentle splash as he entered the water. As he slowly began floating away on some unknown voyage that day, a piece of my heart and soul followed him.

This was my first real experience with death growing up as a child, and it was the most utterly heart-wrenching experience I believe I had ever felt. This, I believe, is because he was the first living thing I truly loved that had ever been taken from me at such a young, impressionable age and in such an absolutely horrible manner.

All my life, I had thought Brownie was more my dad's dog than mine, or any of us kids' anyway, but as I now write this and dredge up all those memories and grief I felt, my heart fills with the pain of his loss, and once again I weep at the loss of Brownie and realize, even though he was the family pet, he was really my pet at that moment in time.

When word got to Mom and my brothers, they weren't mad, just sad and somewhat shocked that such a thing could happen to poor Brownie. Dad, on the other hand, was furious with me. I believe it was more in the fact of how I let Brownie go rather than his death, but I'm sure that he, too, was hurt by his death as well.

Nothing in my mind could have happened at that old house that could have been any more significant than the loss of Brownie, and there wasn't. For the rest of the summer and the following school year, life passed with nothing exciting to talk about.

The following summer came soon enough. I was twelve and leaving the sixth grade. I was finally heading for the seventh grade. This summer, much like the ending of last summer, drummed on without much excitement. Nothing of particular interest happened except this was the summer in which the movie *The Exorcist* debuted.

I think it had actually debuted a year or so earlier in the larger markets around the country. I might have the dates a little goofed up, but it really doesn't matter, as it was the first time anyone I knew saw the movie.

My brothers and their friends were so excited about its arrival ... it was the summer sensation, as I recall. It was all the rage and all they could talk about until they finally went to see it. My mom's sister, Aunt Shirley, who had stayed with us for the summer, wanted to see it as well; especially after hearing Tom and Chris talk about it, but before she got the chance, she had to head back to Tennessee with her kids, Bill and Jodie.

Chris and Tom would tell anyone who would listen how real the movie seemed and how gross and disgusting it had been, even though after seeing it a second time, they laughed during the movie—apparently, it went from spine-chilling to comedy— hmm, how the hell does that work?

They dared people to see it, knowing it would scare the crap out of most who dared to go. But other than my account of Brownie, this was about as exciting as it got while living in that old house. Once again, we were to move to yet another house.

The Old White House on First Street

We wound up moving across town into an old, two-story white house on the south edge of town, commonly known as cow shit flats. With the other homes, we usually moved as soon as summer was over, but for this move, Mom and Dad didn't wait, and it was about the middle of summer when we moved into the old house on the edge of town.

This would be the last house our family moved into before Dad had the old red brick house ready to move into. However, this one particular house was to be where I had one of the best birthdays of my life and also one of the worst summers of my life.

As I'm thinking about it, how completely ironic it seems; on the one hand, I was still innocent, coming of age in a naturally maturing way, and on the other hand, I would have that very same innocence ripped from me in a single stroke by a despicable and insidious piece of putrefied human filth ... and I'm sure these are the man's better qualities, even today. I don't believe it would benefit anyone to say what I really think about the man, but in my mind, once a vile, despicable abomination of human flesh, always a vile, despicable abomination of human flesh.

The rest of the summer went by, and we were all getting used to the house. There was nothing remarkable about it or the location other than there was what we called 'The Pigeon House' next door. This was an old house that was really in fairly decent shape for being abandoned for so long. A couple of friends and

I would go over every so often with our flashlights during the night and pluck pigeons from their roosts. However, we made sure not to take any birds that were nesting with babies or had a clutch of eggs in the nest though.

I had come to love my pigeons, and luckily, our house had cages already set up in the back. So, tending my pigeons was about all I did that summer that was not part of my regular activities. I did let them go before winter came because Dad told me they would freeze if I didn't. So let them go I did, but would start collecting them again when the next spring came around, but again would let them go when we moved the next and final time.

I was still in sixth grade, but I remember pondering what moving up into junior high would be like. I hadn't thought about it before then because I never thought it would happen. But it would happen, and when it did, one of my best memories of that move was my first lunch in junior high.

So, at this time, I do want to digress for a just moment. The reason for this is that I'm not sure I will be able to work this little morsel of memory in at a later time, and I really want to tell it—badly.

It was an unforgettable morning on my first day in seventh grade. I was walking down the hall with my brother Tom, who was in the tenth grade. He explained the details to me of what I must do during lunchtime. He told me that when the lunch bell rings, I need to leave everything where it is and take off running like my ass is on fire, and anything I left on my desk I could pick up before the next class.

Of course, I asked why. He explained that since the cafeteria is in the grade school, it takes time to get outside and up the hill. He went on to explain that if I didn't do this exactly as he said, I would get stuck being the last in line. He went on to say that if I was hungry, I would have to just suffer because the line was always long, and then it would take forever to get my lunch. You see, the junior and senior high schools were connected, and we all ate lunch at the same time and in the same place.

So, I was sitting in my 'pre-lunch' class when all of a sudden, the lunch bell rang … and then it happened. Oh my God, it was like a hundred-yard mad dash to the death! Guys and girls, about 200 of us in all, came pouring out into the halls from the classrooms and then out through the nearest exits. Up the hill, we shot like a stampede of wild buffalo running from a pack of starving hyenas; heaven forbid anyone should trip and fall.

I wasn't the first to make it to the lunchroom that day, but I wasn't the last. I plainly remember thinking how proud I was of myself and the exhilaration of it all, which was at once wild and crazy, and yet a truly wonderful experience. How I will cherish that memory forever, but by the time I was a senior, it really just sucked hind tit, if you know what I mean. Okay, folks, my little detour is over, so I'll return to the story.

It was spring, and school was nearly over. It was my thirteenth birthday on Saturday, the 26th of March 1976. I had slept in that morning because it was Saturday—and my birthday. I was sound asleep in my bed when I turned to roll over but was blocked by something in my arms. I awoke to find my birthday present had been gently tucked under my arms, which Mom placed there while I slept.

I had never asked her for the tennis racquet, but she knew I wanted one because I had been playing the game a lot but had been using Mrs. Gruber's racquet; Mrs. Gruber was my teacher from the fifth grade. She was actually the person who was responsible for getting me hooked on the game when I was in the sixth grade after watching how good I was at playing four-square.

Four-square is a game where you draw a big square on the cement and segment it into four equal parts. One person occupied each square, and a rubber ball or basketball would be batted back and forth to whoever you wanted. If the person receiving the ball missed and it went outside the large square or double bounced, they were out, and each person left tried doing the same to the others. You were also out if you batted the ball out on an empty square.

Again, I digress, but only to explain the game. So, when I looked at the racket in my arms, I stared with utter admiration. I remember thinking how perfect it was as I grabbed it and jumped up from the bed to do a little jig when I hit the floor. I had no idea, however, that Mom had been hiding outside my door watching. When she stepped inside, I hugged her and thanked her so much.

A smile as wide as the Mississippi crept across her face. And little did I know that one of my brothers had taken a picture of it in my arms while I was asleep and another as I did my little happy dance. When you're a little kid, presents really can excite you, but when you're a thirteen-year-old, well, it takes either money or something really big to have that same effect—and this was something big to me.

I thought it was the greatest tennis racquet and the best present in the world; it was made of wood and had a large head and a V-neck. This was near the end of the market for wooden racquets; even cool ones were going out of style to be replaced by steel racquets, which died a quick death to be replaced by aluminum racquets, which are gone today as well.

I believe today, the graphite and composite racquets are the standard. Although many of these types of racquets weren't available then, those that had been were too expensive for Mom to shell out a lot of money on a sport I might or might not stick with. Although, I had been playing since Mrs. Gruber allowed me to use hers at school since I was in the sixth grade.

I loved the game and was always a good player, but I never truly excelled enough to be a great player. My best attribute was my serve, and I was pretty damn good at it, even if I do say so myself. And I actually played all the way through high school and beyond … until I had my accident and couldn't really play anymore.

Although it doesn't seem like such a big deal now, this had been one the best birthdays I can remember as a child, and this wasn't the only present I received on my thirteenth birthday either. The next present would come a few months later, in early June.

My Aunt Shirley was visiting again for the summer, and she was bringing my cousins and our ma'am ma; this was the grandkids' nickname for our mother's mother. Since I was becoming a teenager, Shirley knew it was a special birthday and asked me what I wanted for my present. I didn't want to tell her over the phone, so I told her I didn't know but would figure it out and let her know when she got to Solomon.

I knew exactly what I wanted, but I wasn't sure she would agree with it, especially if I asked her over the phone where I couldn't properly beg her, especially if anyone was around, so I had to wait to do it in person. She was pretty cool about waiting for my answer, but there was also no reason for her to be suspicious either, so now it was a waiting game.

I was like a giddy schoolgirl for at least a week before Aunt Shirley arrived. I wanted to go so badly, and when I finally talked to her, she was hesitant. Actually, she was very hesitant when I asked her if she would take me to see *The Exorcist*. I knew she wanted to go too but hadn't seen it because I asked my cousin, Bill. When he said he didn't think she had, I knew I had a hook, but convincing her wouldn't be easy.

I ended up really having to beg her, as I recall. I pleaded with her, telling her that ever since I had heard everyone talking about it, I wanted to see the dang thing. The hype really suckered me in, and that was all I could think about as far as doing something I knew was out of my reach, but with Aunt Shirley's help, it might just happen.

I had been relentless, though, and eventually, she caved, but only if Mom approved ... of course, there would be a catch, and of course, I begged Mom, but I think she knew she was making a mistake when she finally agreed.

There were a few caveats to her agreeing, however. The first was that I had to figure out how she was going to get me in. The movie was rated R; at that time, R meant seventeen, but I was only thirteen. This one was easily remedied because I knew it was now playing at the 81 Drive-in since it had been over two years since it first came out.

My brothers had been talking about it, telling everyone that it was coming to the '81' as the first movie of the summer, which meant as soon as it was warm enough at night to open. I also knew from experience that I could sneak in if I rode in the car's trunk. We just had to stop about a block away, and I would jump in.

The next caveat was that there would be no screaming allowed. Suffice it to say, I agreed, but I'll tell you that was almost an insurmountable caveat. So Shirley and Mom ended up taking me, my brother Tom, and her oldest son Bill, who was only twelve. Albert, my younger brother, and Jodie, her youngest son, weren't allowed to go, so they stayed home with Ma'am Ma.

So off we were to see the movie. We went to the late show, so people couldn't tell there were two kids in the car watching the movie. When she pulled in, she went to the very back to an isolated spot. When she opened the trunk, we jumped out. Bill jumped into the back seat with Mom, and I jumped into the front with Tom and Shirley.

When the movie began, even from the start, it was chilling, but it became oppressive every time Tubular Bells played; I think they should have been named Hell's Bells, but regardless, they were certainly only the icing on the cake as far as the shock value was concerned.

The *coup de grâce* came once we made it to all the nightmarish shit that seemed so damned real. There was the scene where she was gouging herself with a cross in the nether regions. I was thinking, *What the hell's up with this chick...is she crazy or what?* It seemed so surreal. Then I thought, *Oh my God, could this possibly be true?* After all, this was alleged to be from a true story.

Then there was the freaking flipping and flopping around, like some poor fish that had been thrown onto the riverbank only to suffer from the quivering throws of a suffocating death. And in another scene, she seems to go flying off erratically like some frigging balloon you just popped with a pin. *Oh God! I'm going to freak out,* I thought. *I have to control myself, but this freaking movie is killing me!* and I knew that Shirley and Mom would freak out on me if I couldn't.

I realized about forty-five minutes into the movie that this was going to take every ounce of energy and nerve I had to keep from jumping out of the car and running off screaming across the parking lot like some wild, deranged maniac. I must admit that I didn't scream like Aunt Shirley warned me not to, though.

She could see the terror in my eyes and on my face; I was like a terrified, whimpering little puppy lost in some crazy thunderstorm. She gave me her hand to hold, which, unfortunately for her, was a big mistake. I held it tight, squeezing the piss out of it, actually, but when the real scary shit came on the screen, I would clench, and she would wince. I might add that she finally had to tell me to quit ... and not very nicely.

Although I was scared witless, I couldn't stop watching ... no matter how hard I tried, I just kept watching as if mesmerized by some evil spell. It was like a train wreck, you know, where you are aware of what is going to happen, but you just can't bring yourself to pull your eyes away from the inevitable.

I'm going to tell you, the commercial hype about that frigging movie was nowhere near what it should have been; even my brothers' propaganda paled compared to what they should have been spreading around in their account of the movie. By the end of the show, I was exhausted, both physically and mentally spent. I just wanted to get home where I knew, or at least hoped, it was safe.

In the sum of my very short life, I had never been so completely and unrelentingly petrified; not even to this day has anything had that much power over me. I had been so traumatized by the movie, my friend, that I was unable to sleep for three days straight, and that's God's honest truth. I had believed that this thing that got Regan could somehow get me; it was as if the line between reality and fantasy had somehow blurred in my mind.

I couldn't even sleep with the lights on, and if I had the slightest inkling that I might be falling asleep, I would shake myself or get up and watch television all night. It had been so bad that I was at the swimming pool one day and was in the shallow end sitting on the steps and was utterly terrified that it would get me should I move from where I was sitting; I could just see it coming and entering my body. When I thought that, I would just become paralyzed.

Eventually, sleep deprivation began to take its toll, and I began acting rather buggy and anxious. Mom finally started noticing my odd actions and reactions to things and became suspicious and asked me what the matter was. Till then, I hadn't been about to tell her I was a little chicken shit kid ... nuh-uh, no way. I finally gave in and explained my problem, and guess what? I ended up sleeping with her for the next week or so until the memory slipped far enough away that I could at least sleep by myself with the lights on.

Eventually, I completely overcame the trauma of it all and looking back now, while writing about it, it seems so juvenile, and yet it is funny as hell, and I have to laugh my ass off with each new thought I write. However, my friend, I was nowhere near mature enough to see that frigging movie, which, in my mind, was a damn freak show of epic proportions.

Since then, I have watched the movie quite a few times and have never had anywhere near the reaction I had the first time I watched it. The only effect it has on me is to dredge up old memories of seeing it for the first time at the 81 Drive-in so many years ago—and again, I laugh. Oh, and my cousin Bill wasn't affected at all by the damn thing, and back then, I just wanted to kick his ass because he wasn't.

This, of course, wasn't the most traumatic or final experience I would have while at this old house. I believe the next incident would do more to traumatize me than any other incident to date. In my own mind, it would stigmatize and shame me for the rest of my life—that is, until I began writing this book some years back and let it all go, not to be bothered by it any longer.

Chapter 4

Marauder of Soul

*W*arning: *Although what I have written in this chapter is a true account of an incident that happened to me as a child, some parts might offend some people's sensibilities, especially if they are delicate. I try to limit the vulgarity and graphicness, but in order to help the reader visualize mentally the precarious and absolutely horrendous situation I was in and what occurred, I felt it necessary to use some profanity, and at times, the narrative might even seem pornographic, but please realize, I can't tell how this affected me without telling how I was abused by this person mentally and physically and my reactions and feelings to that treatment.*

It was a Saturday morning in late May or early June of 1976. The windows and front door were open to let the fresh air sweep the stale, musty odor of smoke outside. My parents and most of their friends smoked a lot, especially when drinking coffee, which they had been doing with their friend Jim on this fateful day.

I was becoming bored because all the Saturday morning cartoons had ended, and I was looking forward to going swimming at the Solomon municipal pool as soon as it opened, which wouldn't be until one o'clock in the afternoon. One of the few things the kids in Solomon had to do in the summer was go swimming.

I just thank God there was at least this to keep us entertained during the months we weren't in school. We had other pastimes to help keep us kids occupied, but the pool was where we spent most of our summertime. I believe without it ... well, who knows where many of us kids would have wound up due to having too much free time on our hands—we all know the old saying, 'Idle hands are the devil's workshop.'

I also believe my parents felt the same way because they always bought us kids summer passes so we could go swimming anytime without their permission or needing to get money from them to swim. The pool was basically our nanny during the summer months as we were growing up, and we all enjoyed it very much.

Mom and Dad had been in the kitchen that morning visiting with Jim, an army buddy of Dad's. Jim was a big strapping man, standing maybe six-five or so, and I would guess he probably weighed around two-twentyish. Simply put, he was a large, well-built man who was around thirty years old.

He had dark hair, but not much since he was in the army and had to keep it high and tight. Jim also wore G.I.-issued glasses, which I thought were really quite ugly. There was a peculiar look about him that I didn't much like and didn't want to like. I only knew I didn't care for him when we were first introduced.

As I recall him, I can see him in my mind's eye as clear as day, and I now realize what I didn't like about him; he looked like Jim Nabors ... you know ... Gomer Pyle, U.S.M.C. Gomer Pyle was as goofy looking and as ugly as a mud fence in a rainstorm, and maybe that had been the source of my immediate dislike toward him. I didn't like Gomer Pyle, and I didn't like him. So overall, besides his goofy looks and impressive size, there wasn't anything remarkable about him at all.

Jim had been stationed at Fort Riley Army Base near Junction City, Kansas. I don't know how Mom and Dad came to be acquainted with him, much less became friends with him, as my dad had been retired from the Air Force for about four years. Maybe they had met one day at the commissary, I don't know … and really couldn't have cared less. The point is that this piece of filth was in our lives, my life, and was about to devastate me in a way I could never have imagined.

I was a lanky, bleach-blond kid and was probably average size for my age; I stood about five-two or three and weighed maybe a buck ten. I wouldn't have another growth spurt until I finished eighth grade when I'd nearly reach the height I am now, which is around six-one but would only weigh maybe a buck thirty, which I stayed at until I was nearly through high school.

I would describe myself as a normal Midwestern teen just entering puberty. I was well-liked, and by then, I was a fairly well behaved and generally all-around decent kid who did regular stuff. There should have been no reason for this guy to mark me as anything but a normal, albeit innocent, and rather naïve kid. What were the thought processes leading him to conclude I would be such easy prey or that I would, even in a million years, want to do with him what he did to me? Actually, I don't believe he thought I would be willing to do what he wanted.

While pondering and writing about my recollections of Jim and our association with one another, everything I have learned and know concerning this subject matter is correct as it concerns him and his ilk: Pedophiles tend to prey on innocent, unsuspecting, and trusting children.

These types are usually family members or family friends, or acquaintances. Jim had been associated with my parents for around six months, and I saw him at the house maybe five or six times during that period. So, in essence, we both fit the mold of molester and victim. And since I was the only kid who really knew him, I was the one who ended up being the target of his sick, perverted desires.

Since my parents passed on before I ever started writing this, the only person I've found who recalls him is my mom's oldest friend, Barb Hale. She remembers him, but like me, she doesn't recall his last name, but what can we expect after thirty-five years.

I can still see the whole episode as if it happened only yesterday. I had been surfing the living room channel while waiting for the pool to open. Mom, Dad, and Jim were still having coffee in the kitchen. They were talking and carrying on like adults do, not paying any attention to the kids, or me, as I walked in to get a drink of water. As I headed back to my room to change into my swim shorts, I glanced at the clock, which said almost noon.

While changing, I overheard Jim ask Mom and Dad if I could mow his lawn. My bedroom was just around the corner from the kitchen, so when people were talking normally, I could usually hear what they were saying. Apparently, they didn't mind because Mom hollered for me to come into the kitchen. I remember getting a little excited for just a second and hurried to finish dressing.

I was back in the kitchen within a minute or two, asking what they needed, already knowing what they wanted, of course. Mom told me that Jim asked if I could mow his yard because he was going out of town for the week and was leaving in the morning. Jim then explained how he didn't have the time because he needed to get ready for his trip.

Within a split second, I asked, "How much?" hence the reason for the excitement. Hey, he wasn't my friend or a charity case, so I sure as hell wasn't doing it for free. "How's ten bucks sound?" he asked. Ten bucks was a lot of money back then, and where I'm from and when you're thirteen, ten bucks was considered a nice chunk of change.

I jumped on the offer, and my plans immediately changed from swimming to mowing and making some cash. He had his own mower and gas, which meant I didn't have to haul ours across town to his place, wherever his place was, and this was a problem. When I asked where he lived, he tried giving me directions, but for some reason, I had a brain cramp and just couldn't picture where he was describing—and Solomon was a really small town. I just never went by the area where he lived because I had no reason to.

After a few minutes of getting nowhere with me, Jim offered to show me where he lived once he and my parents were through visiting—was this then a cue for him? I asked how long they would be because I was a little excited about making some cash. Mom said they were about through because she needed to run to the store to get something for supper, and Dad also had other plans. So, I fiddled around for about twenty minutes until Jim finally said he was ready, which was now after twelve.

They said their goodbyes, and Jim and I jumped into his little red Volkswagen Beetle, a cool little car he had purchased that year; to this day, I hate the VW bugs as I find them ugly and totally uninspired. But back then, I told him how I really liked it, and then, out of nowhere, he asked if I knew how to drive. I said, "Yes," of course. I wasn't old enough to drive, and he knew it, but I sure as hell wouldn't let that stop me if he was offering.

Although I didn't have a driver's license, all of us boys knew how to drive at a young age. Growing up in the country our parents taught us for no other reason than they wanted to. Hell, when they started teaching me, I couldn't even touch the pedals, so I had to sit between their legs. Jim and I took a swing out into the country, and I drove for maybe a half hour. He then took the wheel, and we headed back into town to his place.

Looking back, I remember wondering why he was suddenly so nice and friendly. He wanted to know everything about me during our little excursion through the country, and me being so innocent and unsuspecting, gave it up quite easily. I can now see this was part of his grand scheme; befriend and butter me up for what he was either planning on the fly or had planned all along.

When we got to his place, he pulled the mower out from under his trailer ... huh, imagine that, a child rapist who lives in a trailer—go figure. The place was sort of a dump; about ten years old and looking every bit of twenty, or so I thought.

Although Jim was stationed in Fort Riley, about forty miles away, he decided to make Solomon his home for some reason. This was very unfortunate for me because on this day, fate had been cruel, and the hand she dealt me, which was Jim, was total crap; had he not moved to Solomon, I wouldn't have been subjected to this, my ultimate humiliation. But we must all deal with the cards we are dealt, mustn't we.

Before mowing, he checked the oil and topped off the gas. He then started it to make sure it ran. Once it checked out, he showed me where he wanted me to mow. By my calculations, it would only take thirty minutes, forty-five tops. Then after squaring me away, I began mowing, and he went inside.

As I had figured, it took about thirty minutes to finish. I had an incentive for getting the job done quickly, though, I wanted to go spend some of my hard-earned cash on myself at Terrie's drug store, which was the name of the family who owned it at the time. Then my plan was to go to the pool and treat a few of my friends to some ice cream.

As a kid, and even now, I've always enjoyed sharing because it makes me feel good when I do. I believe I got this trait from Mom because she was this way, always willing to give and share if she could.

After I finished, I put the mower away where he kept it stored, then knocked on his door to collect my money. Jim answered in a t-shirt, shorts, and sandals, which was not what he was wearing at Mom and Dad's that morning. I told him I was finished and that I put the mower away. He thanked me and then asked me to step inside, so I assumed he was going to pay me. Once inside, he shut the door behind me. He never inspected my work, though, but I never thought anything about it.

He told me to take a seat on the couch and asked if I wanted something cold to drink. I was a little thirsty and asked if he had a pop. He had some sort of cola and asked if it would be okay. I accepted because refusing would have been disrespectful. He grabbed a glass from the cupboard, put some ice in it, and filled it with cola. He walked back into the living room and handed it to me as he sat on the couch next to me.

When he sat so close, it begged the question, and I asked myself, *Why is he sitting right next to me when there are so many other places to sit?* It was a fleeting thought, and I didn't give it much consideration at that moment.

He then began making small talk and asking questions about this or that, things like how I enjoyed driving in the country. I relented and talked with him for a few minutes but was becoming a little annoyed. I didn't want to sit here and 'chat' with him all day and waste my afternoon. I had plans, and this wasn't part of them.

After about ten or fifteen minutes of meaningless small talk, I couldn't take it anymore and asked for my money … politely, of course. He then asked, "Why are you in such a hurry, Bird?" Of course, I had to explain my plans, but only because I hoped it would help persuade him that I was in a hurry and needed to go. It did anything but persuade him, and this was when he began his slow, subtle, and insidious molestation of me.

He quietly chuckled, then gently placed his hand on my knee. He told me I didn't have to leave so soon and would have a much better time here with him rather than with my friends at the pool, to which I completely disagreed but didn't make a huge issue of it. I didn't get the gist of his comment but wondered what he meant by it. I also didn't want to ask him either since I was in a hurry and afraid it would encourage him to continue.

I became slightly uncomfortable with his remark as it slowly sank into my thick head. I began to realize that it was a very odd comment, and not necessarily because I disagreed with it. The comment, coupled with his hand on my knee, made me feel extremely uncomfortable, and the gravity of its meaning still didn't sink in. I didn't know if this guy was for real or just messing with me. Then, out of the blue, he stood up and said he'd be back in a minute, asking if I was okay before leaving the room.

The thought of telling him that I was not okay or that if I showed any resistance, he might rape me didn't even fire off one single neuron in my mind at the time. And the slightest inkling that he might kill me should I tell him otherwise certainly never reared its head at that moment—I was completely oblivious. However, looking back, the thought of molesting me was certainly on his mind. I can't say it was premeditated, but by then, he knew exactly what he was doing and most certainly what he wanted.

I was becoming a little unhinged, and I'm sure it showed because I didn't know what was going on. When I replied, telling him, "I'm fine," I stammered a little. I wanted to ask him why he was leaving and where he was going, but I was somewhat afraid to, but I didn't know why. Then it dawned on me, and I thought, *He's going to get my money for mowing*, which diffused a lot of the anxiety I was starting to feel.

But before he left the room, and for no apparent reason, he walked over to the front door. Without so much as a word, he turned the lock on the knob, flipped a hasp at the top of the door, and put something through it. I instantly became worried because I was realizing my initial thought was probably wrong. Then an awful feeling set in deep down in my gut, and I remember getting a strong feeling that something was about to happen, and it sure as hell couldn't be good, but I still wasn't sure why.

I was a hundred percent uncertain why he had double-locked the door and was now becoming extremely nervous. My mind was becoming confused, but even so, I immediately began calculating how long it would take me to run to the door, unlock the doorknob, unlock the hasp, open the door, and get the hell out of there, lickity-split. I didn't know why, only that I wanted to get the hell out of there … I was simply becoming seriously afraid for my life.

I had no idea how long he would be gone, though, and I was afraid if he heard me or came back while I was trying to open the door, he would get angry, which would not have bode well for me. Of this, I was absolutely certain, both then and now. I will never know whether he would've done anything violent to me. But I chose to not try to escape.

I honestly have no idea what he might have done had I tried and got caught as I've never been in this kind of predicament before; even today, I can only venture a guess, but I believe one of two things would have happened: One, he either would have beaten me up, and possibly killed me, or two, he would have feigned innocence and gotten pissed that I could accuse him of such a thing, whatever that thing was. Either way, I didn't want a confrontation with him or my parents had he said I accused him of such a thing.

But luckily or not, my instincts had been spot on in not chancing it. No sooner than he left the room did he return. Had I tried, he would not have been gone long enough for me to get the door open and out of the house. Instead, he would have walked right back into the middle of my attempt to escape. But as it so happened, he had walked back in only as I was contemplating an escape, and in my innocence, I still had no idea what it was that I was escaping from, only that he was scaring me.

He had only gone to the bathroom to check on something rather than getting my money as I had originally hoped. I suppose, for whatever reason, I had made the right decision in not trying to flee. But in making this decision, I was to ensure that I would suffer a fate that would haunt me for many years and a dark secret I would keep even longer.

But had I tried, there was at least some small chance that had he caught me fleeing, he wouldn't have tried stopping me. However, this is conjecture and something I'll never know. It's not really relevant either other than to make the observation for you, the reader, because what is, is, and what is ain't gonna change—ever.

As he walked in, he nonchalantly asked how I was doing and if I needed a refill on the pop. My voice shaking and sounding timid, I said, "I'm okay." But my mind was reeling, and he sat down next to me again.

This time, however, he sat much closer and became more aggressive with his advances. Rather than place his hand on my knee as before, he placed it on my bare thigh, just to the inside and closer to my groin than to my knee. Even today, I wonder where this scumbag got his gall.

I felt the coolness from the touch of his hand, and an incredibly weird sensation instantly flushed over my body. I gently gasped. I had tried to stifle it as it came out, but it was a reflex reaction I couldn't cut short, so now it was out there.

Two thoughts arose in my mind at that very moment: One thought was that I finally understood what he was doing, and my second thought was that my gasp probably appeared to him as a gasp of excitement rather than a gasp of horror, which of course it was because of the first thought.

Undoubtedly this is a serious problem when children, or even adults, are being seduced only to end up being raped; every physical reaction that occurs in the body during a fight or flight response, such as dilated pupils, rapid heart rate, shallow, short, or rapid breathing, gasping, or wincing, and yes, even ejaculation, can occur and all can be misconstrued as signs of sexual arousal. When, in fact, they are the body's mechanisms for coping with, or reacting to, the stress of fear—nothing more, nothing less.

Well, my friends, all these signals, except ejaculation, were occurring, and I couldn't do anything but sit there and project. I couldn't say or do anything to stop him as I was completely petrified and unable, so he simply continued as if it were the most natural thing in the world and that in the absence of my refusal, I was enjoying it as much him, only that I was simply nervous toward his advances.

He began gently rubbing my thigh, inching ever so slowly up my leg, getting closer and closer to my groin area. In a single and somewhat hesitant moment, I mounted a brief, albeit feeble, attempt to ward off his advances and defend myself against his lecherous onslaught.

There was a newspaper on the coffee table in front of me, so I picked it up as if I were going to read it. I opened it in a somewhat exaggerated flurry and draped it over my lap, trying to block his hand from moving any closer to my crotch, which was most certainly his destination.

He made some offhanded remark about how I wasn't interested in reading the paper but that I was just teasing him. *Teasing him? Teasing him!* I thought indignantly. *How wrong can this sick, perverted bastard be?* After making the comment, he took the paper from my hand and placed it back on the table, and all I could do was watch helplessly as he did.

My stomach suddenly began churning while my heart skipped a thousand beats, or beat a thousand times, in that split second. I knew full well by then what he was after, and although I had no experience in sex or very little anyway, I was not that naïve.

I couldn't think rationally had my life depended on it, which I thought it did. I was like a sitting duck in a wading pool, and I could do nothing but become a zombie; resistance was not an option.

Trying to fight this man could have killed me because he was far, far bigger and stronger than me. I had no idea what his designs on me were or what his behavioral traits were like; was he a maniac, like some crazed rapist looking for a victim to screw up the ass then beat senseless, or was he a killer who would just as soon wring my neck as look at me if I stepped out of line?

I couldn't outrun him as I was trapped in that old, musty piece of shit trailer and yelling … well, again, I feared he probably would have strangled me to shut me up. All these thoughts, and I'm sure many more, were running through my mind at that moment.

In those days, it wasn't common to hear about these sorts of things happening, and if you did, there was no information available on what to do or what not to do, so you were just totally unprepared to cope should the situation ever arise. Therefore, I just had to sit there at his mercy, praying I would live to see another day. I simply had no idea what to do.

I don't know if this kind of abuse was as common as it seems today. If it were, it was never reported. Maybe it was; hell, for all I know, it may have happened a lot, and if it did, it never went any further than the local news. However, with the media outlets today as techno-savvy and globally well-connected as they are, it only makes reporting much faster and more efficient than it was then, and that's why today we hear so often about it happening.

But just then, this freak show began making his moves with the confidence of a man in complete control. His hand gently massaged my inner thigh as he began working toward my groin.

I couldn't stop him, but I sure as hell didn't have to encourage him, as he was doing a fine job on his own. I just sat there like some bump on a log, being as passive as possible without causing any aggravation whatsoever.

As he started moving closer to my groin, a thought popped into my head, which sank my hopes and scared the shit completely out of me as I thought, *What if I start getting hard?* Not from enjoying it, of course, but because he was playing with me, and I couldn't stop myself from becoming excited, no matter how disgusting this was to me.

Oh my God ... please don't let this happen ... please, please don't let this happen, I begged God. I closed my eyes, and with every breath I took and every ounce of resistance I could muster, I tried not thinking about it, but the more I tried to resist, the harder it became to refuse the urge.

Then, like some vile, slithering snake, his hand moved up my thigh and under my shorts. Without a moment's notice, he slipped under my underwear, gently taking me into his hand. I gasped, then froze.

He began playing with it and gently stroking it. I felt like I was going to pass out from the blood rushing to my head. I sat there motionless ... like a deer caught in headlights. I was stunned. I wanted to jump up and kick his ass, or better yet, kill him and then run, but I couldn't do anything except take it. My heart was pumping wildly, and I was becoming so very frightened.

Then what I prayed wouldn't happen started to happen; I began to get an erection, slight at first, but as he continued fondling me, it was becoming a full-blown hard-on. I knew then that this was all she wrote; for all intents and purposes, I was giving him *carte blanche* to have his way with me. I'm sure he now saw me as a 'willing victim,' if, in fact, there is such a thing.

I was so angry, and I can so clearly remember wanting desperately to cry, but I'd be damned if I was going to give him the satisfaction, and I didn't. I just sat there and let him continue what he was doing, hoping and praying it would all be over soon, but unfortunately, it wasn't—in fact, it was far from over. The mental onslaught of humiliation and physical pain I would be subjected to and have to endure would continue for the next couple of hours, yet seemed like a God-forsaken eternity.

After fondling me for a few minutes, he stood up and drew me up from the couch with him, grabbing my hand. Standing there, staring into my eyes, he asked, "Hey Bird, I have an idea. Would you like to take a shower with me?" But before I could say anything, he informed me that I needed to shower because I had gotten sweaty and dirty from mowing.

I had no idea how to reply to his freaking request, but I asked myself, *Why does he need to shower with me if I'm the only one who's dirty?* Then I realized it was all part of the sick little mind game he was playing, and he was so nauseatingly nice about it, so nice in fact, I wanted to puke my guts up all over him, but that wasn't going to happen.

I was feeling so sick to my stomach, and he was only getting friendlier; looking back, it was as if he was mocking me or something, as I'm sure he wasn't sincere at all. I would rather he just rape me and get it over with rather than act so friendly. Had he done that, at least I could have kept some degree of dignity in the fact that I would have had to take it like the man I was yet to become or die trying.

I knew he was expecting an answer to his question, but the only thing I could accomplish was to shrug my shoulders with my head bowed in a pathetic, half-hearted attempt at trying to express my feelings, which was to simply say, "Hell no!"

All I really wanted at that moment was for this stain of a human to die for what he was doing and what he was going to be doing, which was to control me so that the piece of shit could molest me without any resistance—boy was he a slick, frigging operator. I then thought, *Yeah, right, 'We' need to take a shower … what the fuck!*

Sure, I needed to shower, but not with him, and sure as hell not at his house. So without my dissension or him missing a lick, he grabbed my hand and led me into the bathroom. He was cooing and even a little giddy, acting as if I were his little boyfriend. I believe he was truly enjoying himself and thinking it was as natural as freshly squeezed lemonade.

As we stood in the middle of his bathroom, he began removing his clothes. When he finished, he turned me around, grabbed me from behind, and gave me a little hug. He pulled my shirt up and over my head and threw it in the pile of clothes, his pile of clothes he had just made.

He then spun me back around and, in one fluid motion, knelt in front of me and, with the moves of a pro, unbuttoned then unzipped my shorts. He slowly pulled them to the floor, and I stepped out of them as directed, leaving me clad in only my underwear.

He looked up at my face as he knelt before me and again asked how I was doing and if I was okay. Again, I could only shrug my shoulders in an 'I don't know' gesture. He seemed to want confirmation that I was okay with what he was doing, which he would never get, or maybe it was just a ploy to soothe me.

It was as if he wanted to put an emotional and caring face on the horrible offense he was committing … again, only to keep me under his control. I have wondered sometimes that maybe if I had told him I was uncomfortable, he might have been okay with it and just stopped the whole thing, but I had simply been too frightened to take the chance, so he continued.

With my action or rather inaction, I must have confirmed, in his own mind, my desire to continue, which wasn't desire, only non-defiance. He then slowly slipped my underwear from around my waist and down my legs, where all he found was a flaccid penis just hanging there, almost staring him square in the face as if to say, *Sorry for your luck ... ASS.*

For a moment, I was relieved to see that I wasn't even partially erect, only limp and dangling, but this only lasted a few fleeting moments. He stood up and started the shower, which was soon ready. Standing there naked as a jaybird, he stepped into the shower and offered his hand to assist me. I didn't take it and stepped in on my own.

I was in the front of the tub, and he was in the back. I turned to face forward so I didn't have to look at his naked flesh, especially the thing hanging between his legs, or for him to see mine. Of course, I had already seen his, and even flaccid, it was quite imposing and larger than any other I had ever seen ... not that I had seen a great deal, but when you are a guy, you pee together with other guys, and in doing so, you see a few penises—even at age thirteen. But mostly, I didn't want him to look at me, and I most certainly didn't want to watch him looking at me. As it happened, though, it didn't matter where I stood or how I was oriented; he was all over me.

He grabbed the bar of soap and began washing my backside, lathering me from bottom to top. It was a slow process as he was trying to be what I would now call sensuous; you know, slow, deliberate, soft, and all the while exploring. He made sure he was washing every part of me.

He started at my feet and slid the soap gently between my butt cheeks as he worked his way up. He took it and rubbed it between my legs, slowly working his way forward to the front. He asked me to turn around so he could rinse my back and start washing my front side ... of course, I obeyed.

He repeated his motions, starting from the top of my chest and working his way down to my genitals, where he lingered for a time. He began to slowly lather my crotch, but to my surprise, his actions never aroused me.

Once he had lathered me up, he put the soap down, then turned me around and around, rinsing wherever there were suds. He made sure to get every crack and every crevice that he might've lathered.

When he'd finished washing my body, he began washing my hair. It was then that I began feeling truly violated and utterly ashamed. I began shaking from the total despair I was now feeling. I really didn't know why, and still don't to this day, and I'm surprised he never asked me why I was shaking or why I was so distant and rigid. I think he was too caught up in his own sick, little world to worry about how his twisted behavior affected me.

I didn't know what to do and was so damned afraid I was going to screw up by doing or saying something that would piss him off. I didn't want to react the wrong way, so I sort of let myself go. He wasn't being violent or physically abusive per se, only mentally abusive, so I thought maybe I would get out of this alive if I just played along long enough to get it over with and get out of there.

After washing my hair, he suddenly did something totally foreign to me and took me by complete surprise. He turned me around to face him, and as he did, he knelt in front of me. He looked up at me and took me into his mouth without saying a word. I reacted with a jerk, immediately pulling it out of his mouth while pushing his head away from me, but he had his hands firmly around me and pulled me back toward his face.

I instantly became confused and perfectly embarrassed. *What the hell is he doing?* I thought. I didn't want him to do that, but he was persistent and continued. I just stood there mortified because I'd never done or seen anything like it in any of the few porn mags I'd looked at, but there were no guys in the mags I looked at either, or a man doing this to a woman, let alone a boy.

While fondling me with his mouth, he began sucking. As he did, I got the feeling that I only felt when I touched myself. Although seemingly familiar, the tingling sensation I was now feeling was still very much foreign. I then began to get a full erection, but this time, I couldn't stop myself.

I didn't know what to think and couldn't stop the onslaught of sensations I was having … I was at once excited and yet tormented. *This isn't right; it just isn't,* I thought, but I didn't know how to stop him from arousing me or even stop myself from becoming aroused.

I mean, my God, this man was molesting me, yet I was still getting an erection. The pangs of guilt and shame soon washed over me like a tidal wave—this wasn't right, and I knew it wasn't right, but a part of me felt like it was my fault because I couldn't control myself.

My torment stemmed from the fact that I couldn't stop this little prick of mine from becoming hard, thereby discouraging this big prick, Jim, from seducing me … not that it would have probably mattered anyway. I'm sure he couldn't have cared less whether I was erect or not; he was going to have his way no matter what.

I have since realized it is one thing when you touch yourself because … well, it's you. It's an entirely different thing when someone does it without your consent or even your slightest approval, especially when you don't want them to.

I wanted to run from him and at the same time kick him right in the middle of his head because he was in perfect position, but I just couldn't find it within me; I was simply too frightened. Then all of a sudden, he stopped.

I let out a tiny sigh of relief and began to breathe normally again when he quit. I stood there in all my naked shame, looking down at this smarmy, thirty-something-year-old, wet pervert taking advantage of me, and absolutely had no idea what to do or which way to turn.

Just then, he stood up, standing right in front of me. I looked down to see both of our erections, mine, unfortunately, being way harder than his. He looked down at my erection and made the disturbing comment that put the last nail in my coffin—"It looks like you're sure having fun, Bird."

What was I supposed to say to something like that ... good God, what do you say? I couldn't say a word, for I feared if I did, regardless of what I said, it would only indicate I wanted him to continue. And if I said no ... well, you know the old saying, "Hell hath no fury like a pervert scorned," or something to that effect. I also couldn't find the stamina to resist the assault. I said nothing and turned away, sinking even further into my hopeless shame.

Just then, from behind me, like molten lead pouring into my ears, came the words, "It's my turn now ... are you ready?" My eyes must have become the size of golf balls. I couldn't answer. I was dumbstruck. He asked again, and I knew I had to say or do something, so I turned around.

He stepped to the front of the tub, where the water flowed over his head and down his body. Brushing against his slick, wet body, I immediately stepped to the back of the tub. After turning around, I stared down at my feet and, with my head hung low, asked sheepishly, "What do I need to do?"

With authority, he looked me square in the eyes, then at the bar of soap, and as plain as day, said, "Just what I did for you, of course. Do you want to do that for me, Bird?"

As so many times before, I shrugged my shoulders and, with my usual indifference, nodded in agreement. Just as I began lathering him, the thought dawned on me, *Was he asking me to only wash him, or does he want me to do the other thing and put his dick in my mouth and ... Oh my God! What was he asking? What am I going to do if he wants me to do that gross thing to him?* You can bet I never asked for fear it would give him the idea, and I only hoped he'd never ask me to do it.

I was now in shock from the revelation of it all, and instantly, my mind went numb. I had been slow to soap him up; I lacked conviction or enthusiasm but was only anxious and repulsed.

I started with his shoulders, doing just what he had done to me, and just as I finished his back, he suddenly turned around to have me wash his front. I was stunned by what I saw; his dick went from nearly flaccid and big to erect and huge.

Now when I say huge, it was like a miniature freaking baseball bat; long and stiff. It looked about the size of my forearm but not quite as thick; looking back, I'd say it was about nine or ten inches long with a girth of about five or six inches.

It was so enormous that I couldn't tear my eyes from it, not because I was lured to it, but because I had never seen anything like it before and was mesmerized. The mild trance completely caught me off guard, as I snapped within a few seconds.

Well, that was for sure another green light for him ... it was like going to Jerry's theme park, where he was given free passes to ride all the rides all damn day long. Why the hell would he want to stop now? I'm sure he thought to himself, *Wow! Bird's really enjoying himself...We're going to have some real fun today.* Luckily, nothing more happened than touching his groin area as I washed his front side; I was a bumbling mess doing that.

I was highly relieved that all I had to do was wash him. When we had finished, he turned the water off, and we stepped out of the shower. He grabbed a large towel and began drying me off, as you might expect. When he was finished, I thought he would ask me to dry him off as well, but instead, he dried himself off.

As he was doing this, I thought, *Wow, maybe he only wanted to shower and play around a little. We must be finished.* With this thought in mind, I bent over to pick up my underwear from the clothes pile. But just as I grabbed them, he asked what I was doing.

I told him I was getting dressed. He repeated what he'd told me earlier, "You don't need to get dressed. Put your underwear down, Bird; we're going to have more fun here than you would at the pool." Then, he cryptically added, "The fun is only just beginning, Jerry."

I instantly tensed up and got that old sinking feeling in the pit of my stomach again, which was beginning to churn as if it were making butter, but it was only the taste of bile as it began bubbling up into my throat.

My heart sank because I knew what he intended, but I didn't know what he was going to do and certainly wasn't going to ask. I threw my underwear down. I had only deluded myself by thinking this could possibly be over.

Jim then stood up from the side of the tub where he had been drying himself. Both of us were now standing there naked in the middle of the bathroom, him with a mammoth erection from sensually stroking himself as he dried off with the towel, and me feeling like I was going to hurl at the thought of what lay ahead.

The man was actually going through with his plans—I really had been naïve to think otherwise, but as I was then, I am today, an eternal optimist. He then threw down the towel, grabbed my hand, and led me to his bedroom on the other side of the living room at the other end of the trailer. I could only eye the front door, my exit to freedom, as we walked past it and into his bedroom.

I know that when all these events began to transpire, and as they continued, I was in a state of shock, going from mild to wild as each event occurred in succession, always becoming worse rather than getting better.

Looking back, I see specific events that are very clear when I picture them as a still photograph, but when I let these events play like a movie in my head, it all seems so otherworldly, as if I'm only an unseen observer rather than the actual victim of my own molestation.

No sounds come from our mouths, as if the words I'm hearing are being spoken only inside their heads—no lips moving at all, and I'm only reviewing the scenes as they happen. We never move gracefully from one scene to the next because it's not dynamic or fluid as one might think it should be.

It's like watching some weird, silent movie where the reel revolves slowly as if click-click-clicking through each frame one by one. I know it's bizarre, and I'm sure there is some sort of psycho-babble terminology for this disconnected experience, but I have no other way of describing it.

Inside his bedroom, he sat on the edge of the bed and pulled me in front of him. He was so tall that I hardly had to look down to stare into his eyes—and then, he bent down to take me into his mouth again. As before, he just rolled it around with his tongue, and after a few minutes of this, just as it was becoming hard, he began sucking.

God, there was that feeling again, and this time, there was no fighting it ... I just didn't have it in me anymore to even try. He did this for a few more minutes before taking it out of his mouth and pulling me down to the bed beside him. I just went berserk in my own head.

What was this sick son of a bitch going to do with me or to me? I screamed in my mind. The not knowing was just killing me, but the knowing was even worse. Just as I sat next to him, he sat back and laid himself out like some big, old dog stretching in the sun. So there, this piece of shit was lying right next to me in all his disgraceful repulsiveness. Then, as if he were Mr. Bashful, he softly asked, "Why don't you play with it a little, Jerry? You know, stiffen it up."

God, no ... no, no, no, was all I could think, over and over. He noticed that I was very hesitant and quietly chuckled and said, "It'll be fine. Once you get started and get into it, you'll enjoy it. Trust me, Jerry." To which I thought, *You fucker, I haven't enjoyed anything yet and won't ever ... JIM!* Then another thought flashed in my head, *Why is this piece of shit calling me Jerry ... he always calls me Bird.* I don't know why that bothered me, but it did. I guess first names are more personal than nicknames, and I didn't like it.

I just wanted to stick a knife in this sick fuck's heart, and I wouldn't have thought twice, I swear. I was coming to hate this man more and more as time dragged on. But I relented and very hesitantly put my hand on the huge shaft and started rubbing it a little here and pushing it a little there, just enough to keep him pacified so he didn't get angry with me for not 'playing' along. He knew I wasn't getting into it at all, or maybe he thought I was really stupid because he then put his hand on mine and said, "Here, let me show you how you should do it."

Once my little masturbation lesson was finished, he moved his hand away and told me to try it myself. It was awkward at first, not because I didn't understand the principal, but because of the enormity of the damn thing. Eventually, I got the rhythm of the motion but never showed any enthusiasm in my action.

Within a few minutes of pumping him up and down, he asked me if I wanted to stop. "Yes!" I said immediately, almost enthusiastically. I again thought he might be signaling that he was finished, and as I stood up, he asked what I was doing—well, we all know how this scenario plays out.

I should have known better, but I was going to test him every chance I could, hoping that one of these times he would actually be finished or realize that maybe Bird hates this and wants to leave, so I should probably let him go.

Suddenly, he told me to lay back down next to him. I did but was only going through the motions—doing exactly what I was told, showing no pleasure whatsoever since there was only revulsion.

You know, he never once asked why I wasn't getting into it ... do you reckon he knew why but couldn't give a shit about what his assault was doing to me? I do; in fact, I'm sure of it. He just wanted to get his rocks off, have his jollies with a fresh, young boy, and he couldn't have cared less how I felt. And as for me, I just wanted to get it over and get the fuck out of that hellhole alive—hopefully.

I lay back, right next to him, as he had asked. We were stretched out next to one another; what a pathetic picture it would have been had anyone walked in on us that day and saw us lying buck naked next to one another ... what a pitiful, pitiful sight. He then rolled over on his side and, looking me in the face, reached down and grabbed me again.

However, he was rougher with me this time, and I winced at the pain. I stared blankly at his face as he so eagerly fondled me. I could see this peculiar and strange look in his eyes; today, I know the look to be that of lust as I am many years older and a few years wiser than I was on that day.

After stroking me and playing with my scrotum for a few minutes, he slid down the sheets to align his face with my groin and, in one big gulp, swallowed everything there was to swallow with all the gusto of a starving man at a buffet.

This time, it actually hurt; he was squishing my balls because there wasn't enough room in his mouth for everything, and his teeth had been scraping the shaft of my penis, which was becoming painful.

Eventually, though, Mother Nature took over, and she was as unstoppable as he was. I just lay there staring at the ceiling, wondering when I was going to ejaculate. However, I hadn't even come close to that point when he decided he had had enough of this and came up for air. He looked at me and asked if I wanted to try something 'special.'

I knew I couldn't say no but could ask what, so I did. With an impish grin, he said, "You'll see."

I really didn't like that noise, but quietly replied, "Okay." I just couldn't pretend to guess what he might have in mind for me because I had never been with another person in this manner, let alone a grown man. I could only lay there waiting and wondering in petrified horror.

He told me to stand up for a minute so he could get situated. He threw one leg around me so that I was looking at him spread eagle in front of me. I still had no idea what he was about to ask me to do, but I absolutely hated the scene that was transpiring. Without so much as a 'Here we go,' he swung me around and pulled me toward him. As he steadied me, he slowly positioned me just above and in front of his stiff shaft.

Just then, I reached deep down and, with great difficulty, found the courage to ask him again, "So what are you going to do." This time, he told me in exact terms, and had I had any underwear on, I would have shit them right then and there, metaphorically speaking, of course. As it were, I could only feel despair that I was about to do something I never thought people really did, but only said to degrade someone by calling them a 'butt- fucker' when they were annoying or you wanted to tease them.

I realized at that split second, and to its fullest extent, the ramification of what that moniker truly meant, and except for one time after that, I never used that insult toward anyone. I would cringe whenever I heard someone use it to humiliate, whether from annoyance or referring to a gay person.

Later on, I will give an account of what I did to, and using this insult toward, another person. To this day, it is one of my biggest and most sincere regrets that I will ever have as a child, but which I feel the acts of this man drove me to. In fact, looking back over my life, this is one of the few things I am so unequivocally ashamed of, and I can only pray that the good lord will forgive me.

I suddenly became lightheaded, so I took a deep breath to clear my mind. I had to continue, though, and reached down even further than before to ask him this time, not what he was going to do, but if we really had to do it. He smiled, but not in a nice way; it was an impish grin as if to mock me.

All of a sudden, he became serious and, in a very even, no-nonsense tone, plainly stated, "You really need to try it, Bird, and don't worry, I think you'll like it." Well, that was the end of the discussion, and I surrendered to something I knew I would find repulsive and painful.

My head drooped as I complied and said, "Okay."

I knew this was going to be a bareback ride from, or maybe to, hell. Not that I knew what bareback meant then, but I do today, and it was probably the most demeaning act this psycho-freak bastard could have done to me. Especially considering his size and my total innocence, not to mention my complete loathing of him and what he was doing to me.

I was extremely distressed about doing this sexual act and can remember only praying that he would make quick time of it so that this nightmare would just end. I knew the faster we did it, the quicker I could hopefully get out of there alive and intact.

After he maneuvered me into position between his legs, I heard a big guttural sound come from his throat just before he spat into his hand. I glanced around because I didn't know what was happening, and although I didn't want to be part of it, I was and had to know. As I looked, he was taking the spit wad and smearing it all over his dick. He did it once more; I'm sure it was too big for just one spit wad.

Once he was finished 'lubing' himself, he grabbed my hips and slowly pulled me down to squat just over the head of the thing. God, what was I thinking at that moment? Sometimes I remember with perfect clarity how it made me feel, and sometimes, it's as if there are small gaps in my memory just at critical moments. I guess my mind was just numb at that insane moment.

Suddenly, I could feel the bulging head poking at and wiping across my butt. I immediately regained my faculties at that moment. Of course, I was not going to do this of my own free will, so he would either have to push me onto it or shove it up my ass, but he wasn't getting any freaking help from me.

He continued to gently probe me with the thing, and without so much as a 'Hello!' he shoved it right up into me … "*Oh my god*!" I shrieked. The pain was freaking blinding, and the whole area down there was on fire as he entered me; it was nothing less than total, absolute torture. I screamed bloody murder and yelled at him to stop. I just couldn't take it; even if he had offered me a million dollars, I just couldn't take it.

It was the most awful, excruciating pain I had ever felt, and I immediately jumped up and out of his grasp. Tears came streaming from my eyes and spilled down my cheeks from both the pain and humiliation of it.

Without saying a freaking word, he stood up, put his arms around me, and told me he would be much gentler next time. I screamed, "*Next time*!" but immediately shut up before another peep was uttered, as I didn't want to antagonize him at all. Then the thought popped into my head, *What the hell does he mean … next time?*

He pulled me back onto the bed where I sat shaking like a leaf from the pain, humiliation, and fear. He explained in a very clinical manner that the next time, he would do it in a way that wouldn't hurt. Just then, the thought ran through my head, *Why didn't he do it that way the first time?* but didn't dare ask.

I then asked myself, *How was he going to do it this time so it doesn't hurt?* Knowing he was lying, I remember thinking, *I guess he's just going to rape me and be done with it because he couldn't really care less about me.*

I was sure he knew it would hurt the next time, and so was I … no matter what, it was going to hurt. I then wondered, *How many times and to how many kids has he lied to about this … God?*

Although I don't think it bled at the time, this sick bastard couldn't have cared less that he was tearing my ass apart because he wanted to continue. He also had to know what kind of mental damage he was inflicting on me—he wasn't stupid, just evil.

I could only imagine how many other boys he'd done this to and what they had to endure. Was it the same for them? He acted like an old pro, and I'm absolutely positive I wasn't his first victim.

I didn't know what to do, so I just sat there waiting for the next assault, praying it wouldn't hurt as much the next time as it had the last time. I wondered if his other victims had done as much praying as I did.

He quickly stood up and walked over to his dresser. He opened a drawer and pulled out a jar of something resembling Vaseline. He walked back over to the bed where I was lying and rolled me over onto my stomach. He spread my legs and began lubing me with the greasy crap.

My head shot up, and I asked abruptly, "What're you doing?" but before he answered, he literally shocked the shit right out of me. He began probing me with one of his fingers, gently sliding it inside me, then moving it around and pulling it out.

He then answered, "Oh, don't worry about it, Bird. So how does it feel? Do you like it?"

What do you say to questions like these as you are being violated ... "Oh, sweetheart, I just love it. Can I have some more?" For God's sake, what do you say? Well, I don't know what anyone else would say, but I said, "I don't know ..." as my voice trailed off to a whimper.

This, of course, wasn't true. I freaking hated it; I only said it because it really didn't matter what I said, he was going to do what he wanted, and I didn't want to piss him off.

He then replied, "Good. This will help you relax and lubricate you so it goes in easier." I cringed. I thought I was going to pass out right then and there, but I held on. Maybe it would have been better had I passed out; I would have missed the onslaught of the rest of his little sex capades.

He did this several times, and I just laid there and took it because he certainly had me at a disadvantage. I felt degraded and filthy from his actions when out of the clear blue, I farted. Oh my God, I remember how it had embarrassed the crap right out of me, I wanted to die, but he thought it was funny. He laughed and then went into the bathroom to get some toilet paper. He walked back and wiped my butt with it, all the while laughing like a crazed idiot.

I couldn't even look at him, and I sure as hell wasn't laughing. I just can't truly explain how so thoroughly this man defiled me and how he made me feel—I try, but I can't. Then he stopped laughing and, in a very matter-of-fact tone, said, "You seem to be good and loosened up now," then slapped my butt.

He rolled me back over, lay on his back next to me, and said, "I want you to straddle me." I didn't really understand what he meant, so he explained … and brother, how I didn't want to understand once I did.

I was losing all control of the situation, mentally and physically, and could barely move, but again, I complied with his request. He turned me around so I was facing away from him. He then swung my left leg over him so I was squatting just over his erection. I was surprised to find he was still stiff.

This time, he explained that if I did it myself, I could take my time and work it slowly so it wouldn't hurt. I didn't believe the piece of shit, but obeyed, and sure enough … it didn't freaking help. As soon as that huge thing started to pierce me, I screamed like a raving banshee straight from the bowels of hell as the agony of something so indescribable took over my senses.

I began struggling with him to get loose so I could escape, but he held on, preventing me from jumping off. He began telling me to just go with it and that it would soon feel better once I got used to it. All I could do was scream and scream loudly, all the while begging and struggling to get away. I pleaded with him, "I can't take it; I can't take it! Please stop … just stop!" He hadn't been very forceful in trying to hold onto me, and I wiggled free, or maybe he just let me go.

When he agreed to stop and let me go, I slid onto the bed next to him and lay there whimpering like a scared puppy dog. He tried cuddling me, but I wasn't having any of it. I didn't care if he killed me at that moment—I was done, or so I thought.

I just lay there mortified, staring blankly with my eyes transfixed on the sink. I thought he was finally through, but he only changed gears and wasn't finished with me just yet.

At that moment, my body just sort of went limp, and then I knew this son of a bitch wasn't going to rape me because he said we didn't have to continue. But without missing a lick, he told me that we could do something else instead.

I was about in tears because I thought it was over, but also because I was ashamed of what he had done to me. But I didn't want to add insult to injury by acting like a child, so I bit the tears back. I didn't want to do anything else—I only wanted to quit and go home.

After a few minutes of lying there quietly, allowing me to regain my composure, I suppose, he flipped around without any warning so that our groins were in each other's faces. He immediately began going down on me again, stopping only long enough to suggest that I could do the same thing to him. This wasn't so much a request as an order ... you didn't have to do too much reading between the lines with Jim.

I had two thoughts run through my mind at that moment; the first was how much I didn't want to go down on him, and the second of actually wanting to show my gratitude in some weird, sick way for him not continuing his assault on me.

Funny how shit happens, isn't it? I think he knew exactly how to manipulate me. I would either do it out of gratitude for not ripping me apart and/or because he knew he had me under his control, and I would do it simply because I was deathly scared of not knowing what he might do if I didn't.

For these reasons, I did as he ordered. I hated it, and I hated him, but I did it anyway. I was only able to get the head of the thing into my mouth because it was so frigging big, and anytime it went any further down my throat, I would begin gagging horribly. I hated what I was doing, and I'm sure I wasn't very good at it either, but luckily, it didn't last very long because he didn't last very long.

Within minutes, but what seemed like forever, his pelvis began gyrating, and he started thrusting and moaning, which was the signal that he was having his 'precious' orgasm. Unfortunately, I couldn't read these signals then and didn't know what was happening when his 'stuff' began oozing into my mouth.

I had no idea he was getting ready to unload and didn't pull my mouth from it in time, so I began gagging and retching my guts out when it happened. Luckily for him, there was a sink in his bedroom, which I ran to, choking and foaming at the mouth.

I must have looked like a rabid dog, just spitting and sputtering. My God, I can only recall how awful it was. Once at the sink, I began puking violently. Everything in my mouth and whatever I might've swallowed came out in a big gush. I then began rinsing my mouth out, convulsing and heaving.

Finally, I was finished. I had tears in my eyes, but they weren't from crying; they were from vomiting. He quietly told me to come over and lie down beside him, patting the mattress as if to coax me. I didn't want to, of course, but I felt sick and completely exhausted and had no energy to do anything but surrender to his request. I lay there next to him, dazed and confused for eternity.

I felt a chill come over me as I lay beside him. I thought it was from being sick, but it was the way he kept the trailer. His room was so dark and cold ... he had all the blinds shut, and the air conditioning must have been on high, which I hadn't noticed before.

I eventually worked up the courage to tell him I had to go because my parents would be wondering where I was; of course, he knew this was only a ploy. I also knew that he wouldn't do anything more or harm me physically.

As if giving me his permission, he said that was fine, but before letting me get dressed, he asked if I was going to tell anyone what we had done. He was very slow, calm, and deliberate in his request, which unnerved me.

Of course, I said no. For one thing, he might kill me if I said yes, and for another thing, he knew I meant it because he had so thoroughly shamed me that there was no way I was going to ever tell anybody, which I truly believed at the time. I thought, *I ain't telling anyone anything about this because this fucking secret is going to the grave with me.*

It was probably around four o'clock in the afternoon when I finally left his trailer. I walked outside into the wonderful sun-drenched light of day in all its glory and splendor. I knew I was free of this hideous monster at last.

On my walk of shame home, I realized he never gave me the ten bucks he owed me, and I thought, *There's no way in hell I'm going to go back and get it.* Luckily, Mom never asked about it either because I couldn't produce a single penny to show for it, which meant I didn't have it to begin with, and there would have been many questions raised that I surely didn't want to answer.

I remember how the rage and hate would boil up into my mind, heart, and soul every time I thought about what he'd done to me and how much I hated him for it. I then began scheming in my mind different ways I could get even with him or even kill him if possible, but nothing ever came of those thoughts because I'm incapable of premeditation. However, although I wouldn't go looking for vengeance, I promised myself I would kill him if the chance ever presented itself or if he ever tried doing this to me again.

When I got home, Mom was in the kitchen washing dishes and packing up kitchen stuff. As I walked in and passed through, she asked how everything went at Jim's. I know I had to look like a cat on a hot tin roof, all jittery and nervous. I told her everything was okay and continued heading to my bedroom, not saying another word. I avoided everyone for the rest of the evening, only coming out of my room during supper time.

The next morning, I was still very quiet and reserved, which to Mom meant that I wasn't feeling well; I was always a hyperactive, rambunctious child. She asked again if anything was wrong and if I was okay, and again, I told her I was fine. She felt my forehead to check for a fever—nothing. She watched me for a while as I moped around the house.

I had been utterly traumatized by this bastard, and I know mothers can sense things, but sometimes they ask questions in a manner that is much more direct and far less subtle than the way you wished them to ask.

She took me into the kitchen and sat me at the table. She sat down next to me and, without beating around the bush or skipping a beat, asked, "What's going on, Bird? And don't tell me you're sick because I know you're not." I don't believe the question was meant to refer to the previous day, only knowing something was wrong.

I told her again, emphasizing this time, "I'm fine, Mom."

All of a sudden, this stunned and sort of glazed look came over her face; without pulling any punches and with dead seriousness, she asked, "Did something happen over at Jim's yesterday, Jerry?"

Where in the world did she pull that question from? Oh, my God … she knows something! In the most sincere manner I could muster, I looked at her and said, "No, Mom … nothing happened. I'm fine, I told you."

She just wouldn't stop. She continued asking, only becoming more poignant and far more determined—as if she knew. "Did he try something with you, Jerry? I want the truth." Again, I could only answer as before; there was no way I was going to tell her the truth, whether she already suspected to the point of knowing or even if she tried beating it out of me.

I knew what she would do, and I couldn't stand the thought of her making a big scene, a huge freaking scene, about something I was so absolutely ashamed of and didn't want anyone, not even her, to know about. I could only answer "No" once more, hoping and praying she believed me. She didn't say anything more and told me to go get dressed and go play.

Had I told her what happened, had she heard it straight from my mouth, she would do far more than whatever it was she would end up doing anyway. I'm completely sure it would have made the statewide news; it would've been that damn big. But without absolute confirmation of Jim's acts, her only recourse would have been to tell him to stay the hell away from her and her family ... especially me, or she would kill him ... or die trying, and of this, I have no doubt.

If you knew my mother like I and everyone else in town did, you would know that she would have probably taken a few shots of vodka and then gone over to his trailer and confronted him. It certainly wouldn't have been pretty for her or me, and especially not for him.

As I play the scenario in my head, she would have first taunted him until he came outside, where she would have shamed him right there in his own front yard, in front of God and everyone.

She would've then tried, and probably succeeded, in killing him right there and then ... somehow, some way, she would have surely killed the rat bastard. I've already stated it, and as you become more acquainted with her, you'll see she's not a woman to be trifled with, and if you mess with her, her family, and especially her kids, you will most certainly rue the day.

Jim never came around again, at least not on a friendly basis. Neither Mom nor I ever discussed him again, nor did we say his name out loud. I never heard Dad ask about him or hear him speak Jim's name again, either.

What most likely happened, though, was that Mom talked to Dad then they told Jim to stay the hell away. I truly believe she felt something had happened. And to be truly honest, had she worked at it a little longer and a little harder, she probably would have gotten the truth out of me. This whole damn ordeal drained the life, the fight, and to some degree, the spirit right out of me. But I stood tough and didn't give it up.

Although I never cried tears of emotions during what this man did to me, I hated the very thought of him. I was traumatized for a long time after that but eventually, let it go to hide somewhere deep in the back of my mind, or so I'd like to think, but that is never really the case, is it?

Of course, I kept doing what I always did, which was growing up fast and having fun, only it was very different as I was now stigmatized and carried a scar on my soul where my innocence had been torn from me, and it would take many years for the wound to heal.

I had been non-violently raped, and a marauder of souls had stolen my very innocence. I had dealt with this silently and sometimes angrily through much of my life, only to continue tucking it further to the back of my mind until it didn't hurt so much.

To tell you the truth, as I look back on this experience, I never once panicked while I was so thoroughly defiled that day by Jim; nervous, frightened, anxious, and ashamed, yes, but never panicked, even thinking this man might kill me before or after raping me … I never panicked. However, when he and I meet again, panic will be the only thing on his mind…I'll guarantee that, my friend.

Although I will never forget this incident, ten years ago, I exorcized this demon as I began writing my book and came to accept this part of my life as a part of me, part of who I am, regardless.

In fact, I kept this 'dirty' little secret with me until I befriended an understanding co-worker. Dawn Dreessen was the person, and when I told her I was writing a book, and she asked about what ... well, let's just say it was in and of itself very liberating finally having another human being know this deep, dark thing about me and my past.

Since I first began this undertaking and then put it down, I haven't given 'Jim' much thought until now as I'm once again writing about it and a host of so many other things.

I guess I can truly say I'm pretty much okay today, and writing about it only allows me another opportunity to purge any residue from me (my mind), myself (my heart), and I (my soul). In all honesty, I probably won't give it another thought once this book is written.

Our family finally moved into the old red brick house shortly after this incident, just before school started in the fall of 1976. I was happy to be going into the eighth grade but hated the house. And as I've already stated, Jim and I would cross paths once more, only this time, I was going to make him pray the way he made me, and let me tell you, I would never see him again after our next meeting—I only hope that no other child did, either.

One final word as I conclude this chapter in my life. I want to make one point undeniably clear to you, my reader. When I was a child, this kind of evil act toward children had the somewhat benign yet universal term of child molestation.

I suppose it was, and is, preferred because 'they,' whoever they are, didn't want the thought of this act against children being associated with the more vicious and vulgar term of rape. However, it matters not how you want to paint the picture because regardless of the color of the horse you're painting, it's still a horse, and people need to realize it for what it is, which is rape.

Chapter 5

The Old Red Brick House

We moved from First Street to the Old Red Brick house without much fanfare or trouble. Hell, we had become so used to moving that it was like our family's pastime. The house was located on the corner of old US Highway 40 and Willow Street. This was the house I lived in through half of junior high and all of high school.

This was actually the first home my parents bought when we moved to Solomon. It was the home we lived in before moving to our home that was destroyed by fire. Mom and Dad actually acquired quite a bit of property in Solomon when Dad was in the Air Force. But as time wore on and their drinking became chronic and severe, they would end up steadily squandering the personal wealth they had accumulated through the years.

Had there not been so many strikes against them, they could have continued building on that wealth to eventually make a good life for themselves and their family. But with their bad luck and emotional baggage, compounded by alcoholism and misfortunes from their own doings, their lives were bound to take a harsh path for both obvious and not-so-obvious reasons.

This path would eventually come to bear down on them and their children; combined with our own shortcomings, it would be a long row to hoe for us boys, especially Tom and Albert, who have had the hardest time of it. I want to believe and take some comfort in the possibility that life surely could have been far worse, but realistically, it should have been far better.

I believe this place, the old red brick house, had been the first schoolhouse in Solomon, which speaks volumes about its age and livability, especially since we had moved from it seven or so years prior. Their plans had been to remodel it into our new family home. However, since Dad began gutting it after the fire, the old, decrepit house hadn't been livable for quite some time.

Now, when I say non-livable, I mean it was nearly dilapidated; no running water, no bathroom to speak of, and the kitchen was only a semblance of what a kitchen should be, let alone what it had once been, which wasn't much. The only thing he ever began building was the kitchen cabinets, which were never finished. I don't think he even started building them until we lived on First Street.

Yes, looking back, it would've taken some time, effort, and a fair chunk of money to remodel it into a decent home, and it would have taken an extensive amount of time and a whole lot of money to renovate it into a really nice home. However, at that time, they were still in the financial position to do either, but Dad wasn't one to be rushed, and in so being, he never finished anything concerning the old part.

Why he waited so long to get started remodeling is anyone's guess, as the damn thing had been gutted for at least a couple of years before he even began working on it. So rather than continue paying rent until he was finished, he turned the garage he had added into our makeshift home. So now, he didn't have a place to store his tools or work during the winter, which was why he built the damn garage in the first place. Over time, all his tools were lost, stolen, or ruined from being left in the elements.

Dad was also a tightwad as he only worked when the money became available and only when he could get the supplies cheap; wood that he scrounged; help who worked for beer rather than money; and secondhand anything he could get his hands on.

His trademark became doing everything half-assed, as compared to remodeling our other home, where he built quality into his product. His carpentry skills were better than most; he always worked with pride.

But now it was as if his heart wasn't in it and that he couldn't have cared less … and it was so damn glaringly obvious, but why he became this person is anyone's guess. I can venture a guess, and I'm sure you can too—he simply lost his passion for life and his will to do anything constructive.

So, in changing their plans from remodeling the old red brick part of the house to turning the garage into a makeshift home, it is my most humble opinion that this was one of the most ill-conceived ideas he and Mom could have ever had, but again, they were who they were, and as such, we kids were stuck right in the middle of it with them.

The garage, or home if you will, was completely open and had a cement floor, which he covered with commercial-style vinyl tile that he probably got from the secondhand store. He threw up a wall separating the kitchen and dining area/living room.

He constructed an old rough-hewn wood staircase to the upstairs, where he threw up a few walls here and there to make three bedrooms and a bathroom. There were no doors on any room except for the bathroom.

All of the downstairs walls were clad in plywood—no sheetrock whatsoever. The upstairs outer walls were sheet-rocked but weren't finished, and the inner walls were covered in plywood nailed to studs.

The upstairs flooring was hardwood maple, which was torn out of some old building from who knows where or when, and looked all ratty and tattered, which would have looked fine had it been installed and finished properly, giving it a 'used' charm, but as such it only made it seem completely ill-conceived and trashy.

The exterior siding on the garage was old, used cedar shake shingles he had gotten from God knows where, which was a really odd contrast to the old red brick on the rest of the house. It took him nearly two years after we moved in to even get the sides of the garage covered, which was originally old plywood covered in tar board.

All in all, it was a real shithole of which I could probably say the whole family was ashamed, even Dad—he had to be. I felt so terrible about it that I would ask only my closest friends over as they were the only ones I could trust not to look down their noses or talk to others about it behind my back.

Oh yes, and one more thing, Dad had become a junk collector. He would bring any piece of old junk he could collect home and drop it into the back yard where we kids would have to move it or throw it away, so we could mow the weeds. He would eventually quit this habit once he quit working for the scrap metal company Abilene Metal.

And once the junk was gone, and there was room available, Mom took up gardening and was pretty damn good at it, whereas Dad, on the other hand, decided he was going to raise pigs, which Mom let him. Can you see a pattern emerging here, folks? We were a bunch of Backwoods hillbillies tucked away in the middle of freaking nowhere Kansas.

Some might have said we were 'white trash,' but I can honestly say nobody in Solomon ever acted that way toward us. They may have thought it, but they never acted like it, well, besides Jerry Rock, but he was a dick anyway.

I think sometimes we kids might have felt this way just because of this, but I don't believe we were really ever perceived this way by the townspeople; we had become a very integrated part of the community by this time and were liked by most of the townspeople and tolerated by the rest I suppose.

Confirmation of this is in the fact that all of us boys were involved to some degree or other in both school sports and other extracurricular school activities and programs. And too, it would be my honor that through high school, I would be elected for three years as Student Council representative of my class and Student Council President my Senior Year. I have to believe that if we were truly not considered part of the community, these events wouldn't have ever happened, but they had.

But to somewhat rectify the situation, I renovated the old, run-down shack into a real home with some of the proceeds from my settlement after my accident in 1987, which should've killed me, but would only maim me for life.

I did this for a couple of reasons: One reason was to give something back to the community that helped raise me, and what better way than to remove a serious eyesore. You see, our house was the first thing everyone saw as they drove into town from the East and the last thing they saw as they left town heading East. I know the townspeople had become used to it, but I never would, so I felt the best way to show my appreciation was by transforming the eyesore into something a little more pleasant and respectable.

I tore down the old red brick part of the house. The old 'garage' became the main part of the home to which I added an addition with a carport, and the resulting home was pretty nice, especially compared to what it had been.

The other reason I did it was to give some sense of pride back to my parents and our family. However, within a couple of years, it became too much for Mom to take care of, so I bought them a little one-bedroom home just down the road.

Mom and Dad loved their cozy little cottage, which wasn't much but was just right for them. This would be their final home where they'd find some semblance of peace within themselves and each other and then eventually pass on. I did love my parents, although they could be, and were, exasperating much of the time.

Chapter 6

What's Revenge Got To Do With It

So now, with a little background and tour of the old homestead complete, I will tell you the story of my final run-in with my old nemesis, Jim. It occurred at the old red brick house one fateful day so many years ago when I was just on the cusp of becoming a young man, but without the innocence I had before my encounter with this bastard.

I just don't know why, but for some damn reason, the son of a bitch just wasn't going away or at least wasn't staying away— he was like a bad penny I just couldn't lose. I hadn't seen him since the incident; it was as if he'd gone into hiding, but not on this day. I'd thought he was gone from my life, but apparently, not just yet. Our 'little' confrontation, our last confrontation, occurred not too long after we had moved in when I was still thirteen.

The encounter was brief but explosive, and it wouldn't be long afterward when he would be out of my life once and for all, never to be seen or heard from again—in Solomon, anyway.

I'd tried putting the scumbag away for good that day, but it just didn't work out the way I'd intended; luckily, for his sorry ass, is all I have to say. Had I been a better marksman, this wouldn't have been the case, and who knows where I'd be today had one of the bullets found its mark.

It was a Saturday afternoon. I'd been on my way home from Tim and Tony Betz's. I might have spent the night or been up there visiting; who knows. Summer was just winding down, and the weather was still warm, but I recall it being cooler than usual on that day. I believe it was sometime in September because I was just back in school.

I was walking down Willow Street, happy as a Lark, daydreaming about something or other as kids do at that age. I was about a half block away when looking down the road toward the house, I noticed the very tail end of a car sitting in our drive. I didn't pay much attention as I couldn't see what kind of a car it was or whose it was, but I remember noticing it was red.

With every step I took, the tree line that partially hid the car receded further and further away so that it was becoming completely visible. Within a few more steps, I could make out the back half of the car. I became transfixed because it was becoming increasingly obvious what type of car it was. My heart began pumping faster and faster with each step, and it wasn't long before I knew it was Jim's little red VW bug.

I was now less than a hundred feet from the house, and just as I passed the tree line at the edge of the property, I could see the front door. I immediately became infuriated and thought, *What the hell is this son of a bitch doing at my house?*

By the way, I realize that kids at this age aren't supposed to use profanity like this, but it happens ... believe me.

I then wondered who he would be talking to at my house and what the hell they were talking about. As far as I know, Mom and Dad had ordered him to stay clear of us—although I didn't know this for a fact.

I stopped dead in my tracks right in the middle of the road. I was nearly in a state of panic. *What the hell? What is he doing at my house? Who is he talking to? What are they talking about?* These thoughts raced through my mind repeatedly; it was as if time froze, and the whole world stood still.

I couldn't think of what to do or where to turn. I quickly collected myself and my thoughts and took a couple of deep breaths. Then I began to consider running away. I didn't want to be anywhere near him, especially at my house, even with my family around. But there were no cars, other than his, parked in the drive or on the street.

After a few minutes flew by, I decided to duck into the trees at the edge of the yard to hide and wait; only hoping I'd gone unnoticed. I wanted a place to regroup and figure out what my next move would be. Once I positioned myself in the bushes with a vantage point to the front door, I became aware of it slowly opening. Just then, Jim popped his head out, looking both ways before stepping out of the house.

I again became infuriated at the thought of him being at my house, and my heart started beating uncontrollably, and my stomach felt like a swarm of butterflies had taken off all at once, nearly making me nauseous. However, I do remember thinking it curious that he didn't just step outside but took the time to look around before he did.

I choked back the bile that was rising in my throat. Although he only lived a few blocks away and around the corner, it was always out of sight, out of mind. I never went anywhere near his house because I was afraid to, and I always avoided him like the plague if I saw him anywhere around town, which I rarely did. Again, the thought flew into my mind, *What was he doing at my house?*

I was frightened of him and for a good reason. After stepping out of the house and into his car, I just stood there, hiding under the cover of the trees, watching his every move like a stealthy cat prowling the woods for prey to pounce upon. He just sat there briefly before starting his car, though. What he was doing or thinking, I don't know. Just then, he put the car in reverse and began backing out of the drive.

As soon as he backed out into the road and headed away from me, I shot toward the house. He was heading toward old 40 but was only crawling. I didn't say a word, and apparently, he hadn't noticed me because he was slowly trolling ahead as if in no hurry whatsoever.

I ran into the house, screaming for anyone who might be home. But there was no answer. I looked around as I shot up the stairs to my bedroom, where I kept my hand-me-down semi-automatic 0.22 caliber rifle. I grabbed it from the closet and checked to see if the clip was in it, which meant it was loaded—and it was.

Running from the room with the gun in hand, I kept hollering for someone, anyone, but there was still no answer. I passed the window, looked to see where he was, and noticed he was just sitting at the stop sign. "Perfect," I said to myself as I shot down the stairs to the front door.

I knew he hadn't seen me earlier; otherwise, he wouldn't just be sitting there, but why he was, is only a little mystery never to be known. Or maybe he did see me and was waiting to see if I'd come back out of the house ... who knows?

When I ran out of the house, he'd just made a slow left turn onto the highway and was heading east toward Abilene. His window was down, and his arm was hanging out. It seemed he was listening to country and western on the radio, and it was pretty loud but not too loud to hear me yelling as I ran toward him, screaming like a crazed madman with the gun at my side.

My heart was racing, and my breathing became shallow and rapid. *This man is finally going to pay for what he did to me,* I told myself as I started running. I never ever thought about the consequences my actions might have, but had I, I sure as hell wouldn't have cared. *This son of a bitch is going to die today, and I'm going to be the one who kills him*, I screamed to myself. I had one singular goal in mind, and this was ... you guessed it, to kill him.

He had been about sixty or seventy feet away when he finally noticed me screaming all sorts of foul words and curses. He then turned his head to see me running at him. The gun was in my hand but was still at my side and not aimed. I was now less than fifty feet away and could see he had been startled by my actions. He immediately sped up, but not as fast as I expected, especially with someone screaming bloody murder running at them with a loaded rifle.

Either he didn't see the gun, or it didn't register what was really going down, because if he had, he would have surely torn out of there like someone being chased by an armed and crazed maniac ... which is pretty much what I was at that moment.

As he slowly rolled down the highway, I veered left around the south end of the house to cut him off at the pass and stopped just after making the turn. I raised my rifle to let off a volley of gunfire but was too nervous to aim straight. I believe the first round was probably muffled by the radio. He had turned it up so loud because he still didn't speed up.

I was completely out of my mind by now. I realized I was losing him and began running again, firing randomly at his car. I couldn't take true aim at him because if I had, I would have had to slow down or stop, which would have given him too much time to get away. So, I just kept running and unloading.

I must have hit his car at least two or three times when I believe he finally realized what was happening because he kicked it high just after the second volley and started racing away from me. I was now on the highway but had to stop. I aimed my gun at him and began unloading the rest of the clip; by this time, however, he was too far away—about fifty or sixty yards. I dropped the gun to my side and just went limp. I stood there a minute gasping for air and staring with pure, unadulterated hate as he raced away toward Abilene.

Although the total time that elapsed was only a couple of minutes, nobody ever drove by, which was odd as I later thought about it over and over again. I guess I'm lucky no one had seen me because I would've ended up having to explain what I was doing shooting at him, and then the whole ugly affair would've been out in the open … and it would've been far worse.

Undoubtedly, I would've gone to jail without anything to show for my efforts, except possibly the courts dealing with him, which wasn't nearly the crime back then as it is now. And had I killed him, I would've had the satisfaction of knowing he was dead and my revenge taken. But had I done nothing, I would still have to live knowing he was around, just hiding and waiting.

After the ordeal, I walked back into the house. I was exhausted. I didn't know which end was up because I had just gone through one of the most horrific ordeals barring this monster's rape of my innocence.

I was beside myself from what I'd almost committed upon this man. Although it was out of blind anger, I'd still tried killing this son of a bitch. But as I took the rifle back up to my room, a question ran through my head, *Where the hell is everyone … or anyone?*

As I put the gun away and sat on my bed, I couldn't shake the thought of why no one was home. Jim was in the house, but why was no one home, and why was he in the house? But as I write this, I give it a little more thought, and it begs the question … if no one was home, why the hell was he in my house?

To this day, I can only speculate that he was looking for me. I don't really know why he was, but that's the only conclusion I can come to. He was looking for me to either shut me up permanently or repeat his act of rape on me. With this in mind, I just have to stop thinking about it. I'm only happy knowing that whatever the reason, at least I wasn't there when nobody else was, and then have him walk in and me be totally unprepared and unarmed … what a thought.

I never saw or heard from Jim again after this ordeal. I'm sure he knew that if he stayed in Solomon, he would eventually have to face mine or someone else's wrath for his sins against me. I never said anything to anyone, so nobody knew, or if they did, they never told or talked to me about what I'd done that day.

However, this would not be the last thing that would occur because of what this piece of shit did to me. Unfortunately, what was to happen next time concerning Jim would put another scar upon my soul that I felt was far worse than the actual offense he committed against my innocence.

It would take years, even till after high school, to finally put this man out of my mind and think about other things, good things, and the future. And too, I really think that what kept Jim alive in my mind for that long was the offense I committed against another person sometime after these events. But it wasn't Jim per se, only the sorrow I felt from doing this horrible thing to another person and not realizing till many years later that I had done this because of Jim.

Even after forgetting about Jim, there have been times I've bit back tears of anger, tears of remembrance, and tears of not asking forgiveness from this person for the sins I committed against him, only to feel I will never be able to say I'm sorry for my actions.

Maybe one day I will be able to … and even if he doesn't forgive the actions of a screwed-up young teenager, I can say I asked. As we all know, for every action, there is an equal and opposite reaction. I have tried to live by this rule…but again, we are all human. Mistakes make us human, but what also makes us better humans is that we learn from each of those mistakes and take advantage of those opportunities so we can know, at the end of the day, we are a better person for it.

Chapter 7

An Unforgivable Deed

Autumn finally arrived, and I was settling into the eighth grade just fine. It wasn't much different than Seventh grade; same friends; same teachers; same classrooms ... and so on. I had grown quite a bit in the last five or six months, though.

I was now standing about 5'8" and weighed a respectable 135ish. It would take years for my weight to match my height. I would shoot up another few inches to 6'1" and tip the scale at a whopping 147 pounds before graduating high school. I was becoming tall and spindly with medium-length blond hair and looked like a Kansas surfer dude who'd never seen the ocean in his life.

I had put the shoot 'em up Jim incident and that whole sordid mess behind me and was trying to keep the memories of everything about him at bay. I just wanted to get on with doing what I was doing and moving on with my life. I was a teenager and wanted to focus on school, athletics, and having fun with my friends—not think about him.

Yes, he was lurking somewhere in the back of my mind and would pop into my head every so often, but I simply acted as if nothing ever happened or that I even knew the man. As far as I was concerned, everything was cool.

It was a sunny Sunday morning sometime late in October. I had spent the night with my friends, Tim and Tony, who were identical twins. It took some time to get used to which was which, but eventually, they seemed so different, not only in their looks but their personalities. Even two years later, I still had a little trouble if I saw them from a short distance.

We had been friends for the past few years and became quite close growing up and even into our early thirties. I have since lost contact with them, but I think about them often as we had many good times growing up together. I don't remember how we all became friends, but we'd end up going through much together living in Solomon.

Their sister, Amy, was actually my first girlfriend. She died from leukemia at the tender and innocent young age of twelve years old. She'd been diagnosed before they even moved to Kansas from Minnesota a few years before. I couldn't believe it when it happened, but it was inevitable, considering her condition. The family never lamented her death the way I thought they should or the way I feel my family would have.

Me and my family tend to be emotional people with tender hearts and are inclined to take things like this to heart … on my mom's side anyway. My dad's people are much more reserved and stoic in their emotions, as was my dad. But I didn't have to live with the constant knowing that what was going to happen was exactly what was expected to happen.

I eventually realized they weren't callous but rather time, her condition, and the false hope of recovery from her treatments and the ravaging to her body by those treatments simply made them pragmatic. They'd lived a long time watching her suffer and eventually pass, which must've seemed like a merciful call from God to end the pain and suffering of their loved one and give them a modicum of solace.

She was sweet and kind, and at least I got the privilege of knowing her if but only for a short while before she passed, which was just how it had to be. In her remembrance, I keep a handmade, painted necklace of clay beads she made for me when we dated.

It remains in my treasure chest, and every time I open it and see the necklace, I smile a little and think of her. At thirteen, you just don't know how things should be or how they are going to affect you when they happen, but after all, it is a learn-as-you-go life, isn't it?

Tim, Tony, and I awoke that morning and had cereal or something for breakfast. Tim and I decided to walk around town after breakfast, but Tony didn't join us. We had no plan or idea what we wanted to do or were going to do; we just headed out the door and hit the road walking.

At this juncture, I'd like to interject that because these two were identical twins, I can only say I believe it was Tim and me who went walking and not Tony and I, but as such, in my mind's eye, I see Tim rather than Tony and that is how this memory will play out.

While walking, we talked about stuff that young teenagers talk about … you know, girls, making money mowing, and how to spend it once we made it, but eventually became bored, so we began looking for something to do. Not necessarily looking for trouble or anything in particular, really, only looking to pass the morning without becoming bored to death.

However, what Tim and I did that Sunday morning was absolutely beyond what I believe either of us were capable of doing but did anyway. And so, you know, I want to go on record right now as saying that I take most, if not all, of the responsibility for what happened that day.

Tim played only a small part in helping me commit the horrible act we were to do, but unfortunately, he was part of what transpired, which neither he nor I ever expected to go as far as it did.

We were heading to McKenna's gas station because we wanted a pop while trying to figure out important life decisions, such as how to pass the time. We were just about to Fifth Street and nearing a house everyone in Solomon knew as 'The Wilderness.' It had been named this by its owner, Robert 'Bobby' Poe.

He named it this because the entire yard was like an overgrown jungle of flowers of every size, shape, and color; bushes of every stripe; and every weed known to the state of Kansas, I'm sure.

Bobby had put a sign out in the yard with 'The Wilderness' painted on it ever since his mother had passed. She had apparently passed the home on to him, and since he never had much to do with the yard when she was alive, he probably just let it go and put up the sign so that people would wonder or maybe think this is really how he liked it to look.

Bobby was probably around thirty-something, a recluse, and a bit eccentric. Although a loner, he wasn't necessarily disliked by the townspeople but only had one friend to his name in Solomon that I'm aware of anyway. His name was James Harris. I say he didn't have any friends save one; I don't know this for sure because he was always riding his bike to Abilene, weather permitting. So, he may have known people there, but if he did, they never visited him in Solomon.

James was an odd fellow. He had very similar traits to Bobby, only he was in his early to mid-twenties, and I think this is why they got along so well. One was just a younger version of the other; where one saw how he was, the other saw how he would be. James and Bobby became close buddies over time, so much so that eventually, a rumor would emerge that they were lovers.

I don't know if this was true, but I do know that Bobby took James in when he appeared one day, apparently having nowhere else to turn. Why James showed up and why Bobby befriended him is anyone's guess.

I know neither would harm a fly, but they were an easy mark for ignorant kids when spotted riding their bikes around town together. Not that we'd taunt them, but we did make rude, vulgar comments about them amongst ourselves, but not always. As I grew older and took a different view of life, I began talking with Bobby but never with James.

But on this particular day, they weren't together when I noticed James leaving Bobby's yard on his bike as Tim and I headed to get a bottle of pop. Bobby must've ridden to Abilene because his bike was gone. If he were there, he'd have either been riding it with James, or it would've been sitting in the front yard or on the front porch as usual.

It wasn't uncommon to see James riding alone around town, though, but when he was, it usually meant he was going fishing. And this is what he was doing that day. His pole was strapped to his back, and his tackle box was in hand. He was having a hell of a time navigating through the yard, though, since he was only steering with one hand. I remember how funny it was watching him wobble across the yard, and I pointed it out to Tim. We were about a hundred feet away when James saw us looking and laughing at him.

He'd just made it onto the road when he noticed our laughing. As soon as he steadied his bike, he stopped and hopped off. We could see he was embarrassed and gave us a scathing look as if we were being mean to him. We really weren't being mean; we just thought it was funny because he looked like a clown with all the gear he had and the wobbling he was doing. That's the only reason we were laughing.

Tim and I kept heading down the street when out of nowhere, I hollered at James, "Hey, James? Where'd you learn how to ride a bike?" And then, without even thinking, I added, "At clown school." Both Tim and I began laughing. I was only joking, of course, but James didn't take it so well. He was embarrassed and thought we were teasing him, compounding his anxiety.

He headed toward us, and we met at the intersection. James, totally offended by now, asked, "Why are you guys laughing at me?" I explained to him as nicely as I could, but he just kept accusing us of being mean to him. It was no big deal to us, so Tim and I kept walking. James started to follow.

This was when something came over me, and I turned to James and said angrily, "Get the fuck away from us, you fag!"

This was the first time I'd ever used this word in an angry, non-joking manner. I'd always used it when teasing someone, but never to be mean. Hell, I barely knew what it meant until Jim had molested me. Then I knew exactly what the whole gay lexicon really meant.

Tim then said, "Why don't you just get the hell out of here and go fishing, James."

But after what I said, James was incensed and told me bluntly, "I ain't no fag ... Bird turd." My nickname was Bird ever since I was a little baby, and calling me bird turd would piss me smooth the fuck off, and I mean, right now ... nobody ever called me that and got away with it, well, mostly anyway.

I'd never backed down from a fight with anyone if they got me to a point where I couldn't control myself, regardless of their size. However, I remember that James was at least ten years older than me and just about my size … maybe a little taller. And although I was a kid, I wasn't stupid … James might know a little more than Tim or me about fighting.

I didn't want to get my ass kicked that morning, so I only looked at him and said flatly, "Don't ever call me that again, James!" I was as serious as a heart attack, and he knew it, but I did make the first comment after all.

Tim and I just kept walking, but James didn't follow. Then, out of the blue and for no reason, feelings of hate and rage boiled up inside me. I began shaking uncontrollably, and my mind went blank. Just then, without so much as a peep, I spun around and lunged at James as he'd just gotten on his bike and began heading the other way.

Tim yelled, "What the fuck, Bird! What are you doing?" I didn't answer, though. All I wanted to do was hurt this guy and hurt him badly. At first, Tim thought I was just going to smack James around a little … you know, teach him a lesson, so Tim joined the fray.

He began holding James' arms while I smacked him a few times, but then it was as if I became possessed, and something evil took hold of me. I literally began stomping the shit right out of James. I felt like I wanted to kill him. I went totally berserk and lost all control of my senses. Whatever it was, though, it blindsided me as much as I blindsided James.

When I started kicking James and punching him in his gut, Tim let him go. James dropped to the street with his hands wrapped around his knees. I was cussing him all the while I was hitting him. James began screaming and crying.

He put his arms over his head and, while crying, yelled, "You can't hurt me, you can't. My body is strong, and it will protect me from you! It will protect me!" The more he cried out, the harder I kicked and hit. While crying, he begged me to stop, telling me his body was strong and would protect him ... his body would protect him.

Tim got scared. He yelled at me to stop. The more he yelled, the harder I hit James, punching him in his head and back, then alternating between kicking him anywhere I could land a foot—in his head, his ass, or anywhere—I just wanted to kill him. I screamed into his ear, "I'm going to beat the shit out of you, you butt-fucking queer!"

Finally, Tim yelled, "Stop, Bird! *Stop it!* You're killing him, and someone is going to see us. Stop ... *please*!" He then grabbed me and yanked me up from James. He screamed, "We have to leave ... *now*!" As I looked at his face, then into his eyes, I could see the fright, and I snapped to and instantly realized what I had done and became scared myself.

I stopped and then took another few seconds to see what kind of damage and pain I'd caused James, but without a second thought, I took off running like a freaking wild animal being chased by something that would tear it to shreds if caught.

Tim followed as we ran for the park about a block and a half away. When we got there, we ran into the gazebo, where we crouched down to hide. We hid there for a while, waiting for things to blow over ... just in case someone did see us and what we did. We then began discussing what had happened and trying to find the answer to why we did it, but really, why I did it.

There was no answer to be found, however, it would have to be pondered for many years and take a little more wisdom than either of us had at the time. And before I realized why I did what I did and the consequences my actions would have upon my soul, again, I pushed it to the back of my mind, as I'm sure Tim probably did and never gave it another thought.

The whole episode lasted only five minutes, but it was long enough to hurt James seriously. Before we ran, I looked at his body, the body I had utterly whaled upon. I could see the blood around his ear running down his neck. There were red welts all over his arms and face. God only knows what other harm I'd caused the poor man; broken ribs, ruptured kidney ... who knows. My God, I've never done anything as heinous to anyone as I did to James that Sunday morning so many years ago ... and I was only thirteen at the time.

After about thirty minutes, or at least long enough for the mess to blow over, or so we thought, we left the park. We knew we couldn't go back near the scene of the crime, which was only about two blocks from either of our houses, so we headed downtown.

Being Sunday, downtown Solomon was deserted. But still, Tim and I kept it on the down-low, so we walked through the alley rather than chance walking down Main Street. No sooner than we began our trek to the other end of town, which was only a block away, did we see a car coming over the tracks, again, about a block away and in the direction we were heading.

We knew it couldn't be good because it was the city cop, Bill Tegtmeyer. Bill was a very large, imposing man. He stood at least six-one or two and weighed at least 250 pounds; he reminds me of John Candy in as much as they look very similar in size and looks but without the happy-go-lucky disposition. Bill was all business and no fun whatsoever, but what do you expect from a police chief? And Tim and I were sure he was looking for us.

We were too far down the alley to return the way we came. There were buildings on both sides for about a quarter of a block, so we couldn't just dodge to the side. We had to run to the open field about a hundred feet ahead. The only problem was that the car would probably pass by the alley before we made it, but it was our only avenue of escape.

We shot up the alley and fled into the field just as the car passed the alley. If we were lucky, he hadn't seen us and would keep going. Hunched down in the weeds, we waited a few minutes and … nothing. Just as we thought we were in the clear, he parked twenty feet away in the alley.

Bill stepped out of his car, and we could see him looking around. Although the weeds kept us hidden, we knew that he knew we were there. Suddenly, as he paced back and forth in front of his car, he yelled loudly, "McMillan, Betz, I know you're hiding. You need to get out here, and I mean now." Tim and I looked at one another and, as if reading each other's minds, knew we were caught and what we had to do.

But before we could rise or answer, he continued, "If you don't come out here now, I'm going to go see your parents, and it's only going to be worse than if you come out now."

We stood up with heads hung low because we knew why he was there and what we were in for.

Apparently, someone had seen what we did to James and called him. Bill then read us the riot act for what we did. He was very loud and very scary. He got right down in our faces with finger-pointing all the while. However, and for whatever reason, I'll never know, he didn't take us in or tell our parents.

He only made us promise never to do it again. However, this was only upon the condition that we never did this kind of shenanigan again—ever again. If we did, he promised to throw the book at us. He also promised that if we ever messed with James again in any way, we'd wish we were in hell rather than Solomon because this was his town, and he could do whatever the hell he wanted to us. I could've pissed my pants right then and there, and it was all we could do to shake our heads in agreement.

I don't know why he never did anything other than read us the riot act. Maybe it was that James took off, so all he had to go on was what the witness told him rather than actually seeing the proof by all the marks I had inflicted on him. Regardless, we were grateful, and I've never done anything like it since, and I'm fairly certain Tim hasn't either.

Although what I did was as wrong as wrong can be, it wasn't until much later that I pondered on it enough to realize that what Jim did to me was why I did what I did to James. It was because of Jim—plain and simple. I took all my frustrations, hate, and pain Jim caused me and inflicted it on James. In essence, I turned James into Jim in my mind.

But what hurts me the worst about the whole ordeal is that I know the suffering Jim caused me and that I could deal with it, but the pain and insults and sheer hate I inflicted on James … what did this do to him?

The crux of the problem is that I don't know how I made James feel; what kind of emotional torment from the pure unadulterated degradation did I cause him? Could he cope with it the way I did with Jim … or was it that a thirteen-year-old could make a twenty-something-year-old man feel such pain and hurt … could he ever forgive me for doing such a horrible, evil thing to him for no reason at all and even more so, can I forgive myself for doing such a thing to such an innocent person?

The more I thought about this, the more I became upset with myself for doing such a thing, and this touched my soul in a way I wouldn't have ever thought it could in a million years. I was actually having a harder time coping with this ordeal than the ordeal I went through with Jim.

However, in doing some soul-searching throughout my life, I realized that what I did to James was only a reaction to what Jim did to me. Somehow I had to deal with what I did and get over it, emotionally anyway, so I could move on.

I did, and I have, but there will always be a mark on my soul that I can only hope the man upstairs can forgive me for. I was only a child when I did this and have since realized I am not, nor have I ever been, the person I was at that moment.

I believe that at the end of the day, it is not that we do bad or wrong things, it's that we realize what we did was wrong; that we ask forgiveness and we learn from and correct them; that we humble ourselves so we can move on to become better and wiser than that person we were at that moment. I believe that then, and only then, can we continue living and growing mentally, physically, and spiritually ... you know ... the way we are supposed to.

Chapter 8

First Flight of Fancy: The UFO Incident

There are times in our lives when we have lapses; lapses in judgment; lapses in morality; lapses in memory ... and sometimes, we have unexplainable lapses with no rhyme or reason. It's simply an 'anomaly' of nature that sometimes happens when our minds are faced with critical decisions or unexplainable events. We try to rationalize our decisions and compartmentalize the unexplainable into a mental frame of reference where none really exists.

And sometimes, as this occurs, a chemical imbalance might arise that causes our neural synapses to misfire or hyper-fire. Unfortunately, our higher mental capacities and cognitive abilities, such as reasoning, might diminish considerably when this happens.

Should this occur, it might be possible for a benign situation to seem fantastic or too great a thing to overcome, but in reality, it isn't as insurmountable as we imagine. We then may become totally irrational, almost to the point of mental incapacitation, because our cognitive self, our mind, has basically locked up on us.

It might become so debilitating to our rational self that our autonomic nervous system kicks in, and our instincts, rational or not, take over. This may then evoke highly emotional responses where no response, or a completely different response, is required. And if this synaptic misfire goes unchecked and into a feedback loop, we might then do things that seem totally absurd to everyone but ourselves, which then might cause ourselves or others harm.

So why the lesson in psychophysiology, you ask, well, first off, this is probably pseudo-psychobabble at best, but as such, it helps me describe something I really don't understand. And the reason for the lesson is because of my best friend, Bob Houser, which, even today, I still grapple with trying to fathom why he did what he did so many years ago.

Growing up through grade school and junior high, Bob was normal, fun-loving, and as rascally a kid as any other kid in school. However, there were instances during high school and even beyond that things began to change ... although slowly, the changes went 'mostly' unnoticed, or maybe ignored, even until the end of his life, which I will explain later in another chapter of my life.

Bob and I had been best friends all through school, and even today, I believe we would still be if it weren't for a most untimely yet planned death—his death—when he committed suicide at age 24. Looking back, I can see the tell-tale signs taking place over a period of time as he began his slow transformation from fun-loving, easy-going Bob to angry, depressed, and suicidal Bob.

Except for possibly one occasion before his suicide, which was near devastating, his actions would seem maybe odd at times, but not really so far out that anyone except the most astute psychologist would attribute them to suicidal behavior; kids and even adults can be easily given to flights of fancy or moments of high anxiety and excitability.

But as I began working on my book and looking at these separate events as one event transpiring over time, I can see a pattern emerge; the odd behavior points to something more, something dangerous and possibly even mental instability. However, I won't be able to follow each of these behavioral incidents because that could be a book unto itself. Therefore, I will only give a few highlights prior to his suicide.

Now, I'm no shrink or anything remotely related to a therapist type, but I am a scientist. I have been trained to recognize patterns when I study data and observe events. Therefore, I know when something is wrong, and let me tell you … something was wrong with Bob, but unfortunately, it was only after the fact that the pattern becomes obvious to those who investigate, and then only if you are looking at it as I have.

It's like looking at a flood on the ground compared to seeing it from an airplane far above. Yes, you see the water that surrounds you when it surrounds you, and it would certainly seem bad, but when you view it from above, all at once, it's simply overwhelming … not only to you but to everyone and everything engulfed by it.

The same holds true for Bob; we saw little pieces of his odd behavior here and there because he was near us, and honestly, at times, his behavior might have gone beyond odd. But I, nor anyone else, ever saw the whole picture until it played out over time and was viewed from 'above' as a single, continuous event. And it was certainly devastating, not only to him but everyone whose life he touched—just like the flood.

His final act of desperation, which caused such a deluge of raw, unadulterated emotions, left each of us wondering why and how such a horrific thing could ever happen to such a well-liked and loved young man … and so the story of my best friend, Bob, begins.

It was a clear, moonless evening sometime in the summer of 1977, just before entering high school. Bob, Steve, and I had been walking the streets this night, a frequent pastime for us kids. The stars were bright and shimmering like twinkling white lights on a Christmas tree. It seemed as if the entire Milky Way could be seen from almost any vantage point you wished to stare at it from.

Solomon was the type of town where you could run the streets at night because nobody was ever out to tell you otherwise. You only had to be able to get out of the house without being noticed or telling your parents you were going to a friend's and then be home by a certain time.

Steve Morris, a member of our little band of merry men (and women), was fifteen, the same age as Bob. And although we were different ages, we had always been friends since I could remember.

I still see Steve occasionally when I go back to Solomon to visit my old stomping grounds. He hasn't changed much and probably never will. He's worked at the same place as far back as I can remember. His dark, black bushy hair and beard and mustache all look the same as they did 20 years ago, except for the gray. Steve's a decent guy, and he certainly means well.

We had been walking and talking that night about nothing really out of the ordinary or very interesting, as I recall; maybe we were planning a hiking adventure in the country, which was also one of our frequent summer distractions. We'd just turned the corner onto Sixth Street and were in front of the swimming pool. We were heading toward Bob's house, which was only a block away.

There were no porch lights on anywhere. The houses were mostly dark except for a few inside lights that were still on; some people left kitchen lights on as night lights, or people were watching the ten o'clock news or Johnny Carson ... or whatever the hell old people did back then at ten o'clock at night. But this was how Solomon was and probably still is today because, well, it's Solomon.

All I know is that it had been past ten o'clock, and once we passed the pool, it was dark except for the starlight and the afterglow from the pool lights. They kept the pool fairly well-lit ever since a handful of midnight bandits broke in and raided the ice cream freezer that was never locked and then took a midnight dip, but we won't discuss this little delinquency as it might tend to incriminate the 'not so innocent' and his unlikely posse of merry men (and women).

We had walked far enough past the pool to see the stars again, and with each step, the night was getting darker, and the stars were getting brighter, and the crickets were singing their little chirping song that was so much a part of those slow, simple summer nights so long ago.

We had reached maybe a hundred feet past the pool when Steve and I noticed Bob had fallen behind to stargaze, or at least that's what he appeared to be doing. He was maybe twenty feet behind us when we stopped to see what he was doing.

No sooner than we turned around to see him staring skyward, he threw his arm into the air, pointed to something in the sky, and hollered, "Look, guys, look at that light up there." He didn't seem overly excited about it, showing little more than a slight interest.

Steve and I turned our heads, following where he was pointing in the sky. Not seeing anything, Steve asked, "What are you looking at, Bob? I don't see anything."

Bob then asked, "Do you see it, Bird? It's right there, just above the trees."

I looked at Steve, shrugged my shoulders, then turned and asked, somewhat confused, "I don't see anything, Bob. What the hell are you looking at?"

Instantly, Bob ran up to Steve and me. This time with more conviction, he said, "It just went behind the trees." He began showing us the light's route since he first saw it less than a minute ago. He said excitedly, "It was right there. You guys didn't see it?"

We looked at each other, then at Bob, and in unison, flatly stated, "No."

"Man, it was fast and huge. It was like a glowing ball of light, and it shot from there to there." We watched his hand trace a path across the sky. I could see he was now getting a little agitated. It was as if he thought we should have seen what he saw, or maybe we did but were screwing with him. It wasn't worth mentioning that we disagreed because it didn't seem like such a big deal. However, Steve and I were getting a little freaked out as his persistence grew.

At that moment, we were standing between Bob and the destination he'd said the light had headed for when all of a sudden, without any notice, his eyes grew to the size of ping-pong balls, and his mouth flew open wide. He screamed, "Son of a bitch, there it is again!" This time, he pushed past us and launched down the street, screaming, "It's a flying saucer! Shit, guys, it's a freaking UFO! Come on, guys, we've got to tell someone!"

Being a little dumbstruck by his sudden outburst, Steve and I exchanged uncertain glances. We then turned back to look skyward at where he had been staring and pointing. As we quickly scanned the sky, I asked, "Do you see anything, Steve?"

Bewildered, he replied, "No, man, I don't see anything." Without thinking or saying anything, I turned and took off after Bob ... Steve wasn't far behind, though, but he wasn't as fast as me, so it took him a few seconds to catch up.

Within seconds, Bob was about halfway down the block when he veered off the road to the left and ran directly up onto Mrs. Werner's porch; hers was the first house with a light on inside. Still following, I watched him shoot up the stairs and wondered, actually half yelling, "What the hell is he doing?"

Just then, he started pounding on the door. I stopped so fast I nearly flipped head over heels right there in the middle of the damn street. Within seconds, Steve was next to me. Gasping for air, he grabbed my shoulder and asked the same thing I did, only much quieter.

I replied, "I have no idea, dude! He's freaking nuts!"

He was acting like some bizarre and crazed wild man. He then began begging frantically, "Open the door! Please ... please, someone open up the door!" Steve and I were on the verge of having our own freak-out as we watched the scene.

We sure as hell weren't running up there with him, so we ducked behind the bushes next to her porch. We began whispering as loudly as we could, telling him to stop it and to come on. He never heard us, though, because he was caught up in the moment; it was as if he had completely lost his mind. Suddenly, the porch light came on as Mrs. Werner answered the door.

Mrs. Werner was the town's librarian, a straight-laced yet friendly old woman who was not easily given to excitability and didn't much like to put up with it. She was probably in her mid to late sixties, so her reaction was far more subdued than what Bob hoped for in a response.

"What's going on, Bobby Houser?" she asked matter-of-factly. Bob was rather frantic at the moment like he had more than a touch of the 'cat on a hot tin roof' syndrome that I had way back when.

He was pacing around, pointing toward the sky, when, in a fevered pitch, he began telling her what he'd seen in the sky. Really though, it sounded like one long, confusing run-on sentence without punctuation to separate thoughts or highlight important things, which made him sound like he was foaming at the mouth as he continued spitting out the words.

He implored her to see what he was talking about, to let him show her his discovery. However, in the middle of his rant, Mrs. Werner firmly interrupted, "My goodness Bobby, do you know what time it is, son?" All the while not really paying him any attention whatsoever.

Emphatically, Bob exclaimed, "I don't care what time it is, Mrs. Werner! There's a huge glowing light in the sky! You need to come out and see it … Pleeeease!" he implored.

Mrs. Werner, in all her grace and goodness, looked at Bob and flatly stated in a no-nonsense manner, "You need to get home now, Bobby Houser. I don't want to hear anything more about some light in the sky. Now get going, or I'll call your parents."

Without hesitation or missing a lick, Bob sprung gracefully off the porch like a gazelle leaping from a craggy ledge. When he landed, he flew directly across the street. Steve and I watched for a few seconds until Mrs. Werner, shaking her head as if somewhat bemused … or confused, stepped back inside, and shut the door. Steve and I took off after him as soon as the light went off.

He had run onto the porch of another house and repeated his performance as Steve and I hid next door and watched. We tried motioning for him to come to us but without success. We then pleaded, "Let's go, Bob! Come on, let's go!" But he looked at us as if he were looking through us. There was just no calming him or trying to get him under control. Then the porch light came on, and a man opened the door.

However, this time, the resident wasn't nearly as friendly as Mrs. Werner. When Bob started his tirade, the man yelled, "You just shut up!" Then, in no uncertain terms, told him he had better get off his property and shut his 'you know what' mouth, or he would shut it for him. Apparently, he didn't have a great appreciation or patience for being awakened by the pounding and ranting of a crazed teenage boy.

Bob's initial outburst of high anxiety had finally passed, and he simply ran out into the street where he stood hunched over, hands on knees, panting like a dog after chasing a rabbit. He just couldn't believe no one would listen to him, let alone believe him. He began swearing up and down that what he saw was real.

"It was real, guys, it was a big, bright light, and it moved like nothing I'd ever seen before. I swear. It was fast, and then it was gone," he said in a somewhat conciliatory manner. He then explained how the thing went from here to there instantly and seemed to stop on a dime before shooting off again.

He kept searching the sky for whatever he thought he had seen, or maybe what he did see, but to no avail as it never reappeared, making him feel even more like we didn't believe him.

While calming down, he kept looking for the light that he, and only he, had seen that night. We all began gazing up into the dark abyss of the night sky, looking at the stars. After a few minutes, Steve pointed and said, "There ... look, there! Is that what you saw, Bob?" We all looked and soon found what Steve was pointing at.

It was a small light moving across the night sky in a slow, constant fashion. Bob adamantly stated, "NO! No, no, no, that's not what I saw!" We all knew it was a jet moving across the sky, but hey, at the time, it was the only thing that remotely fit his description. Bob settled down within the hour, and it became as if the ordeal had never happened.

We never talked about it again. In fact, it only occurred to me when I began picking my brains for the memories I wish to share with you. But once I began thinking about this and other things as they concerned Bob, I noticed some incidents make a little more sense now than when they occurred—as to why they happened anyway—and maybe they weren't just things kids do because of over-active imaginations.

Chapter 9

A Fragile Mind

The next incident occurred just before finishing our sophomore year or early summer, just before our junior year in high school. This incident gave everyone pause and reason to question if something might seriously be wrong with Bob, questioning his mental health.

Bob was definitely given to flights of fancy, as I've already established, and he will further solidify this later on in another incident, but on this particular occasion, what do you call it when someone, for no apparent reason, tries to commit suicide … certainly not a 'flight of fancy.' And, as I will also discuss, there wasn't any 'apparent' reason to believe he had any motive whatsoever to do this foolish thing in the first place—regardless of what the 'experts' said. However, as I later found out, this initial assumption of mine wasn't necessarily correct.

The way I saw it then, it was anyone's guess as to why he did what he did, that the experts got it completely wrong. Although it would take another seven years for him to try again and another four months to actually commit the shocking act, I'm sure it wasn't due to the reason they gave on this occasion, and maybe it wasn't until long after he actually went through with it that the true reason may have come to light. The following are mine and Sheri's accounts of what transpired so many years ago; however, there are a few points we sort of disagree on, and I will explain both when they come up.

Sheri was, and is still today, a tall, lanky woman with flowing red hair and a freckled, fair complexion; her mother called her freckles 'angel kisses.' Even today, she is a beautiful woman who has aged quite gracefully. She is my age, and at the time, we were both sixteen and sophomores in high school. More than a few years before, Sheri had become part of our little posse after moving to Solomon when she and I began hanging around while Bob, Steve, and I also hung around.

At the time of this incident, Sheri and Bob had been dating for maybe a year or so. To be honest, I despised that they ever became involved. I was jealous, and I hated it. I felt that I was in love with her and that if she was going to be with anyone, it should be me, not Bob. I had known her first and had been her best guy friend since she moved to Solomon in the sixth grade.

I thought I was so in love with her during our freshman year, I began writing a song in her honor during Mrs. Hansman's music class. I titled it 'Somehow everything really is Forever' or 'Sheri F.' for short. The F is the first letter of her maiden name, Fairchild.

I never finished the song, though, because it wasn't very long after I started writing it I found out she and Bob were together and lost all interest in it. I suppose then I wasn't as in love as I really thought because I would've finished it had I been.

Mrs. Warner, the school librarian, not Mrs. Werner, the town's librarian, who Bob ranted like a madman to earlier, was Mrs. Hansman's assistant pianist in music class. She had helped me write the music for my song, but I had written the words. I don't recall what happened to the unfinished sheet music, but I'm sure it will never be found, and I'm absolutely sure it will never be forgotten … as long as I live.

I'm also sure Mrs. Warner got a hell of a kick out of helping a love-struck teenager write a love song. As I recall, it wasn't too bad a piece of work, and we enjoyed attempting to do something we had never tried before.

Eventually, I got over the fact that they were together and would be a couple for many years to come. I only had to accept the fact that she and I would only be the best of friends and nothing more. I did accept this, though, knowing it would rip our little group and friendships apart if I didn't, so I eventually let it go.

I still have a picture of her from the ninth grade that I keep in my treasure chest, and, as with Amy's necklace, I look at it every time I open the chest for whatever reason. It always brings back memories of when things were more carefree and life was much grander than it sometimes seems now that I'm a lot older and far more jaded.

Sheri had been home in the afternoon, and God only knows where I was at the time as it was so long ago, and I find it somewhat hard to remember. I do know where Bob was when I found out what happened a few hours after the ordeal occurred; he was at the hospital getting his stomach pumped.

Apparently, Sheri wanted to talk to Bob sometime that day, so she walked across the street to his house. They were neighbors and had been since Sheri moved to Solomon. Since she was a family friend and Bob's girlfriend, she walked inside without knocking.

She found Bob's two younger sisters, Amy, and Julie, watching TV in the living room, and asked what was going on and if Bob was at home. Without so much as a hello, they told her he was in the bathroom.

Amy and Julie weren't much at small talk, especially when glued to the TV. When Sheri asked how long he would be, the girls replied they didn't know, but he'd already been in there a long time.

Sheri walked to the bathroom, just off the living room, and knocked on the door. "Hey Bob, how long are you going to be? I need to talk to you." But there was no answer. She waited a minute or so, then knocked again.

This time he answered, "I'll be out shortly. Just wait in the living room."

After some time had passed, Sheri walked back over to the bathroom and asked through the door, "What are you doing? Are you taking a bath or something?" Again, he didn't answer. She was getting a little irritated because there wasn't a peep out of him. The girls hadn't noticed the conversation, or lack thereof, between them as they were engrossed in the TV. She knocked again, but this time with more insistence.

Just after she began knocking again, Bob opened the door and walked out. Sheri described to me that Bob appeared a little wobbly and acted somewhat distant. She asked him what was going on, to which Bob didn't reply. He simply walked past her and into the kitchen, where he started rifling through the cabinets as if he were looking for something.

Sheri asked what he was looking for, and Bob mumbled, "Don't you worry about it. It's none of your business."

She again asked if he were okay because he seemed distant and confused.

About that time, he began staring at her as if she weren't even there. He started to say something when a grimace crossed his face as he doubled over in pain. She leapt over to grab him, thinking he was going to hit the floor. But rather than fall, he only began heaving as if trying to throw something up, but nothing came out except the drool from his mouth.

Sheri screamed for Amy and Julie to help her get him to a chair. The girls ran in and helped sit him down at the kitchen table. Sheri was now extremely worried. She knew something was wrong but wasn't sure what it was.

Bob then started frothing at the mouth and gagging. He began talking incoherently. Sheri and the girls then became distraught and began frantically asking him what was going on. Within seconds, the thought hit Sheri like a ton of bricks that something was really wrong.

As Sheri put two and two together, a thought dawned on her. She then shot into the bathroom. She opened the medicine cabinet but didn't see anything out of the ordinary, but then she gave a cursory glance around the floor and then the trash can next to the toilet. She grabbed it up and began searching its contents. Just then, her heart momentarily stopped and took a nosedive straight down to the pit of her stomach as she found empty bottles of all sorts of medicines.

She screamed and frantically began asking Amy and Julie, "Where're your brothers? Where are Kenny and Gilbert? Amy ... where are they?" She knew Jim and Dee, Bob's parents, weren't home.

Amy, not really grasping what was going on and in a mild state of panic herself, screamed back, "I don't know! But I think Gilbert's in bed!"

Then Julie, also not really in tune with what was happening, asked in a somewhat mystified and timid tone, "What's going on, Sheri?" But there was no response, as Sheri was already heading to Gilbert's bedroom.

Without hesitating, Sheri shot toward Gilbert's bedroom with the wastebasket in hand; Gilbert had worked the night shift at the truck stop and was sleeping in that morning. She threw open the door and screamed at Gilbert to get up. She was shoving the basket in his face while frantically telling him Bob had overdosed.

Still half asleep, Gilbert didn't react with cat-like reflexes but was soon in the kitchen wearing only his skivvies and a t-shirt. He began shaking Bob and asking him questions, trying to gauge how alert or out of it he was. By now, Bob had become even less responsive and coherent. Gilbert tried shaking and talking to him but wasn't getting any kind of clear answers to his questions.

Gilbert at once ran to the bedroom and threw on his clothes. He shot back out to the kitchen, where he and Sheri whisked Bob out of the house and into Gilbert's car. They took off like a bat out of hell heading for Memorial Hospital in Abilene. Within twenty minutes, they were in the emergency room, where Bob was rushed off to get his stomach pumped.

The medical staff began asking what kind of pills he had taken. In their rush to get to the hospital, they forgot to grab the empty bottles. Sheri called the house for the medical staff, and Julie answered. She then read the names of the medicines off to the nurse.

The bottom line here was that he had taken enough of the meds that, although they weren't deadly in small doses and on their own, the quantity and interaction of the medicines could have done serious harm to him had he not gotten to the hospital when he did.

They eventually got him pumped and irrigated, but he wasn't completely out of the woods yet since there were still many medications in his system. They kept him over for a day or two to monitor his progress until he was released into his parent's care.

Jim and Dee didn't take the matter lightly, though, and decided that Bob needed to be psychologically evaluated by professionals. I believe they sent him to the Menninger Foundation mental hospital in Topeka, Kansas, for evaluation. This was pretty serious as the Menninger is highly respected and one of the foremost psychological institutions in the country, if not the world. You would hope that if a mental problem led to this behavior, they could surely find it.

Bob was 'evaluated' for an extended period, then released. Hoping they wouldn't find him insane or something, which, of course, was not the case, it was determined that Bob, like many kids his age, was only looking for attention. Well, I can only say that if this was true, he sure couldn't have found a better way of getting it. The only problem was that he wasn't looking for attention from his family, only his girlfriend, Sheri.

The problem was that the doctors never diagnosed the root cause, only the symptoms. Sheri had just previously broken up with Bob. I don't know if he discussed this with his doctors or if anyone explained this to them. What they didn't realize then, as I do today, was that he was madly in love with Sheri, and he couldn't stand the thought of her breaking up with him, that she might forever leave his life.

I'm fairly certain that in his own mind, the only way to ensure she would never leave him was to demonstrate that he had the ability to kill himself if she ever tried again. He now had that power and would hold it over her until the day he sealed his own fate with the headstone of his grave. However, I will add that he never actually said this to me, as it's only my personal hypothesis.

Therefore, rather than show the ultimate expression of love in that he was willing to give up his life for her, all it really accomplished was to bind them together in an extremely unhealthy and eventually unhappy relationship, which would take its toll on them, thereby eventually destroying himself. The man was completely and utterly mad about her, and it would possess him unimaginably until he died.

I'm not saying his possessiveness was the cause of his suicide. Thousands upon thousands of men are jilted daily by the women they love and adore. Yet regardless of the reasons or what they believe the reasons to be, they don't kill themselves because of it. There had to be a root cause, a cause other than hormones run amok. There had to be another, more disturbing reason: Chemical, biological, mental, or otherwise, but again, we will never really know.

Sheri, and the eventual loss of her love, may have simply been a trigger mechanism he nurtured through the years that would develop into something far more troubling. Something that when the time came, or when he couldn't take life any longer, he would use as the imperative to commit his final act of desperation.

Maybe it's better not knowing what compelled him to go through with something so shocking when he must have felt all hope was lost—or there was no hope to begin with.

As I've stated before, this was only the first demonstration of his ability to venture into a place so dark and forbidding that most would never consider visiting. His next attempt, and then his subsequent death, will be far more shocking and horrifying than this, his initial attempt at committing something most of us would never consider, even in a million years.

So, with that being said, the following is my account of Bob's next flight of fancy, which again illustrates that something more might be going on other than a rush of hormonal volatility.

Chapter 10

Second Flight of Fancy: The Alien Incident

It was a warm, clear evening the following summer after Bob's attempted suicide. It was the summer before our senior year in high school … the summer when Bob decided school wasn't for him, finishing only his junior year.

Whenever I asked why, the only reason he would give was because he wanted to, which wasn't much of a reason, but I let it go at that. I'm sure he had reasons for quitting school and for not telling me why. I guess it just wasn't what he really wanted to do. Nevertheless, on this particular evening, school wasn't on our minds when we got together and went cruising.

Beatrice Kay Dowell, BK for short, was at Sheri's that evening; BK was another member of our little clique who had joined the crew in junior high. She was tall like Sheri but without the freckles. She had long, wavy brown hair and was a hoot to boot.

She was a sweetheart, but like many of our friends from school, we've simply lost contact throughout the years. I did see her once when we ran into each other at Worlds of Fun in Kansas City, but nothing much transpired from the encounter.

On that night, as the evening wore on, Bob, Steve, and I also ended up at Sheri's. Sheri's mom, Carol, who was divorced, had been working that night at the Truck Stop. She was a fuel desk clerk on the evening shift, which made Sheri's the perfect hangout for our young posse.

We were all sitting around shooting the breeze and becoming bored when Sheri suggested we go cruising; nobody disagreed, and if they had, they were going home. However, since it was Steve's parent's vehicle—an International SUV, I think—he had to agree, which he did, of course, so we all jumped into the truck and headed out.

Steve and BK were in the front, and Sheri, Bob, and I were in the back. Not long after we left Sheri's, BK, being BK, asked Steve if she could drive. Of course, Steve agreed, so he stopped, BK took the helm, and Sheri sat up front with her.

Now, even though we were teenagers, we didn't really drink. However, we did smoke cigarettes. I don't think any of us had even really smoked pot … we may have tried it, but it wasn't something we did at all regularly. So, I'm fairly certain we were all sober and straight as an arrow on this night.

We were chatting about who knows what and having a good time just cruising the streets when, out of nowhere, BK asked, "Hey guys, you want to have a Chinese fire drill?" Although we were having a good time, she wanted to kick it up a notch to liven things up. It was later in the evening and had become dark, adding to the thrill of a Chinese fire drill.

Everyone agreed in unison. "Where should we have it?" she asked.

We began mulling over the question when I said, "Wherever we decide, it has to be outside of town."

Everyone agreed but kept discussing the 'where' when Sheri exclaimed, "How about the Sand Curves?" to which everyone happily agreed.

The Sand Curves is a sandy stretch of winding dirt road about a mile and a half long just southwest of Solomon. To get onto it from town, you first have to pass over an old steel bridge with wooden planks covering the deck, which was bumpy and would creak and thump when you drove over it.

It spanned the Solomon River and was nicknamed 'Rickety-Rack' because it was so old and, well, rickety. It was sort of the portal to a wonderful place many teens used for partying, making out, and simply having fun during the summer.

With everyone in agreement, we headed west down main street, then out of town until we reached the end of the road. This is where if you turn left, you head directly over the bridge and onto the curves; if you turn right, you head toward the railroad tracks and back into the west end of town. BK stopped the car and asked, "Everyone still cool with this?"

"Yes," was again the consensus.

She turned left and slowly crept over the bridge. It was now fully dark with only the stars and headlights to illuminate the way; really though, without the headlights, you couldn't see a thing even if it were in front of you and staring you right in the face or until your eyes adjusted anyway, and even then, it was still pitch dark.

As we crossed the bridge and got to the other side, BK sped up. At about fifty yards or so past the bridge, she slammed on the brakes without any notice. No sooner than the car stopped, she yelled, "Chinese fire drill!" slammed the car into park and jumped out.

Without hesitation, everyone else sitting by the door jumped out too. We were all running wildly around the car like a bunch of raging lunatics … nearly running one another over as we passed during our mad dash around the car.

Sheri, Steve, and I had been sitting next to the doors while Bob was stuck in the middle between me and Steve. Within seconds everyone had made it out, around, and back into the car—except for Bob.

If you've ever had a Chinese fire drill, you know that everyone runs one way or the other, which can be awkward as you try to miss those running toward you. Regardless of the way you go, you have to run all the way around the car and get back into the door you leaped from, and too bad for the last person still outside because they get left behind.

Because Bob was the last one out, he jumped right into the middle of the fray and seemed baffled as to which way to run … in this game, hesitation is definitely your enemy. Everyone else made it back to their door, jumped inside, and shut them. However, BK punched the gas before Bob could reach his door to jump inside. This, of course, ensured that he'd be the loser and, therefore, the unlucky bastard who got left behind.

We sped off, heading down the road while leaving Bob standing in the glare of red taillights and a swirl of smoky, brown dust. The only thing we could see as we turned to watch him fade into the distance was the look of utter surprise and total confusion on his face. Within seconds, we couldn't see anything, not even his silhouette in the shadows that consumed the dusty red light as we flew further down the road.

BK was heading full tilt down toward the T. The T was located about a mile away at the end of the curves, where we would turn around. "Wow!" BK exclaimed. "Bob really sucks at this, man!" At which we all began laughing. Knowing you weren't the unlucky sucker who got left behind was an exhilarating feeling.

Once at the T, we decided to stop and have a quick cigarette … and, you know, to give Bob a little time to realize just how bad it sucked losing at this game, especially in the country at night. We then began feeling bad about leaving him, though, and before finishing our smokes, Sheri said, "I feel kind of bad, guys. We should go back and pick him up." We all agreed, and within a few minutes, we were back to where we'd started.

We couldn't have been gone more than ten minutes at the most, but as we began slowing down where we left him, he was nowhere to be found. "Where the hell is he?" I asked, somewhat perplexed.

Steve replied, "I don't know, man. This is where we left him, wasn't it, BK?"

"I'm sure it is," she replied hesitantly.

We were nearly at the bridge when Sheri said, "Turn around, BK. I think we might've dropped him off further back."

To which Steve then made the point, "He should be here somewhere, Sheri. It doesn't matter if we let him off here or there. He should've been waiting for us when he saw our lights."

Sheri tersely replied, "I know Steve, but he's not here, so what the fuck?"

It was getting a little tense, and BK turned on the dome light. As she did, she glanced at me. I gave her a worried look to imply, *this is fucking weird,* to which I could see she agreed.

"Maybe he decided to walk back to town, guys," I said, trying to ease the tension, then added, "Head over the bridge, BK, and let's see if he's walking down main."

Everyone agreed.

Main Street was the street we came out on and runs about a third of a mile along the river between the bridge and the town, so it's sort of like being in the country since it's a dirt road and there are no houses, buildings, or lamps to light the way.

Everyone agreed, and BK headed back to town. Just as we passed over the bridge and turned right onto main, Bob sprang out of the ditch where he'd been hiding in a thicket of bushes and weeds. BK slammed on the brakes and screamed, "What the fuck, Bob!" as he lunged in front of the stopped truck like a wild beast being pursued by a hungry lion looking for supper.

He slammed his hands onto the hood and began screaming, "Where the fuck have you guys been?" repeatedly. It was obvious he was in a state of panic. I then noticed he was bawling; tears were streaming down his face.

Steve immediately opened his door, but before he could step out to let him in, Bob jumped headfirst across Steve's lap, all the while screaming, "Go! Go! Go! Get the fuck out of here now!" It didn't take a boot upside her head for BK to realize something was wrong, and she punched it. All of a sudden, we went careening down the road toward town with Bob's legs still dangling out of Steve's door and his head resting squarely in my lap.

He was completely beside himself, shaking like a leaf with tears rolling down his cheeks. You could see the fear in his eyes and hear the desperation in his crackling voice. We were all yelling from being in a mild state of panic, and though barely coherent, the general theme from above the ruckus was that he was scaring the shit out of us and what the fuck was going on.

Within minutes, we were cruising through town. Bob had begun settling down enough to explain what had happened as we calmed down. The details of his account would create quite a stir amongst us. However, I can't answer the question as to whether this was just a scared guy's flight of fancy or if it might have actually been a symptom of something far more serious.

Although the chatter was still thick, the excitement was replaced by an awkward calmness. Just then, Sheri turned to look at Bob, who was trying to get situated between me and Steve in the back seat. In no uncertain terms, she, as direct and serious as she possibly could, asked, "What the frig, Bobby? What's going on with you? And why are you freaking out like this? Damn it, Bob, you're scaring the shit out of us!"

The questions were fired in rapid succession with little, if any, pause between them. Everyone immediately shut up because we were afraid of both egging on a fight between the two and, like Sheri, had a real desire to know just what the hell happened in the few minutes we were gone.

Bob had shut off the waterworks and finished wiping the tears from his face, then wiping his nose with his hand, asked stiffly, "Why the hell did you guys leave me like that, Sheri?"

Sheri countered, "It's a freaking game, Bob, that's why it's called a Chinese fire drill. And you lost!"

Somewhat taken aback by Sheri's direct harshness, Bob began telling us his story with his composure mostly intact. "Fine, I'll tell you, but you're not going to believe me when I do," he stated flatly. He seemed to have a twinge of guilt hidden somewhere in his earnestness, though. "After you guys took off, I stood there waiting, thinking you were just going down the road a little ways to turn around and come back and get me. I waited and waited before I decided to screw it and headed back to town."

But as he continued, his voice began cracking as if he were getting choked up. "I thought you guys really left me." He then turned away from the group as I believe he didn't want to make eye contact with anyone for fear he would begin crying again.

You could see the ambivalence in his face and hear the reluctance in his strained voice. He didn't want to continue but knew that we wouldn't just let it go.

He knew we not only wanted but needed to know, so he continued, "It was so dark outside once you guys passed the first curve, and your taillights disappeared. I got a little scared and decided to walk back to town, figuring you would pick me up on your way. I headed over the bridge, and just as I made it to the other side, something happened."

He immediately paused as he was trying to keep from choking up. Instantly, we all asked, "Then what? What happened?" as if we were listening to some old, scary radio show, like the CBS Mystery Theater, and could only anticipate what he was going to say next.

Bob found it in himself to continue. This time, he took a deep breath and let it out before he started. "I just made it over the bridge when I heard something behind me. It wasn't loud or anything, just a weird noise." Bob was now calm and confident enough to continue as if he were telling a creepy story around a campfire.

"I slowed down just as I made it over the bridge. I was afraid to turn around, though. I was afraid because I was alone and it was so dark. I didn't want to run either. I thought if it were a wild dog or coyote, it would start chasing me and then attack me."

Then Steve echoed Sheri's question, "So why the hell did you hide in the bushes, Bob?" Then he added, "If it were a dog or coyote, it would smell you there anyway."

To which Bob snapped, "I'm getting there, Steve. Just shut up and listen, damn it!"

By now, we were all hanging on Bob's every word as he continued, "Like I said, I'd just got across the bridge when I heard something. I slowed down but kept walking. I was trying to hear if it was really something moving or just my imagination. Maybe it was just the rustle of some leaves."

"I couldn't hear anything but my own footsteps, so I stopped. I knew if I stopped, I could listen more closely. I thought it was only my imagination, but when I stopped, I made the freaking mistake of turning around. Oh, shit, was that a damn mistake or what! God, Sheri, it was there in the middle of the bridge ... right there in the middle of the fucking bridge!"

He was nearly in a panic again, but Sheri, in a soothing way, prodded him to continue, "Come on, Bob, you're with us, and there's nothing around now—nothing."

He paused briefly, trying to regain his composure. Once he did, he began again, "When I turned around and looked back over the bridge, it was standing right there in the middle. It was just looking at me, you guys. I swear I couldn't move or say a word. It was looking right at me, staring at me, and it wasn't moving at all ... just staring at me."

BK chimed in, all excited, "What the hell was it, man?" She stared intently in her rearview mirror to watch Bob's every facial expression.

"Watch the damn road, BK! You're going to kill us," I said as she drifted uncomfortably close to the curb. I then turned toward Bob and asked, "What was it, Bob? Come on, tell us. What the hell was it?" I was as curious as anyone in the car and knew he needed urging to continue.

"I don't know what it was or didn't at first, and hell, maybe still don't know ... but then it started coming toward me, not running, just heading toward me. I couldn't move. I felt paralyzed." He then covered his eyes with his hands. We could see he was terrified by the thought of remembering whatever it was.

He then told us, and was as dead serious as he could possibly be, "It was a fucking alien man ... can you imagine that? I think it was a fucking alien." Then, in a fit of nervousness, he screamed, "*It was a freaking alien, man!*"

He sat back from leaning forward and began laughing in an obsessed, maniacal sort of way. Then, no sooner had he started laughing, he stopped and then, after a minute or two, calmly repeated, "It was a freaking alien, okay. Are you happy now that I've told you?" Each of us got an instant case of the creeps and were astonished.

We immediately shut up, except for Bob, who was trying to calm down. We then began searching each other's faces looking for clues to gauge how each of the others felt. Then Steve, in total disbelief, said, "Really? I think you're full of shit, Bob. There wasn't no freaking alien chasing you!"

Then BK interjected, "What the hell. Are you crazy or what, man?"

"It's true, you assholes. Why would I frigging lie about something like this? Tell me ... why?"

Sheri and I just looked at one another. Then, in total sincerity, she asked, "What did it look like, Bob?"

"Well, it was so dark I couldn't really tell. I don't think it was tall, and ... I don't know, it was so freaking dark. But I know one thing for sure: its eyes were gigantic, yellow, and glowing ... I swear, you guys have to believe me. But I knew you wouldn't. I shouldn't have said anything." He then stared out the window, not looking at anyone.

I then asked, "If it was so dark, Bob, how could you tell it was an alien and how big it was?"

To which he answered, "I just could, Bird. I guess my eyes had adjusted to the darkness. I don't know. It was just there, right in front of me, and then it started walking toward me from about twenty-five feet away.

"That's when I snapped to. I guess my instincts took over, and I took off. Just as I got around the corner, I couldn't see it, so I jumped into the bushes. I kept watching it, praying it wouldn't see me until it disappeared in the trees across the road."

"Wow-wee, Bob! I exclaimed, then after pausing, said, "That's a hell of a story, dude! You know, you might have been chased, but I'm sure it wasn't by no freaking alien." I paused again, then added, "Maybe it was a Bobcat ... or something else, Bob, but not an alien."

I hated to say it because it was like I didn't believe him, and I really didn't, but I said it anyway. Then after my comment, the conversation changed to everyone discussing whether or not it could have been a Bobcat or something else.

Here's where I have to interject that Sheri believes he said it was a Bobcat and that maybe I had asked sarcastically, "Are you sure it wasn't an alien, Bob?" referring to his previous 'encounter' with the UFO. However, if I had said that, I would have surely added something to the effect of, "You know, maybe he was left here by the UFO you saw when we were kids."

And, too, had I made that comment, they would've sure been fighting words, but it never came to that. I have to say that in my mind, I remember it as I've written it, and if I'm wrong, I certainly want to apologize to Sheri. I have asked Steve about it, though, but he doesn't remember much about the incident as it was so long ago, and it didn't mean as much to him as it did to me.

Eventually, everyone, except for Bob, of course, agreed that must have been what it was—a Bobcat. Concerned, Sheri then asked, "Are you okay? Are you hurt or anything?" There wasn't a scratch on him, only a bruised ego at our denying his claim. But not only did he honestly believe he was chased by an alien that night, he thought he actually saw the damn thing, or at least its eyes.

Bob could only shake his head in disagreement with our decision that it was a Bobcat. He then muttered under his breath as he stared out the window, "It wasn't a Bobcat, you assholes … I know what I saw, and it wasn't a freaking animal."

We continued riding around for a while longer. We talked about it and discussed it, but he never changed his mind or ours about what he thought he saw. BK stopped at her house, where we dropped her off, and Steve dropped the rest of us at our houses. And like before, once we stopped talking about it, it would never be mentioned again, until now anyway.

As I think about it and the more I remember these things that happened so many years ago during the course of my friendship with Bob, the more compelled I feel to write them down, the closer I get to writing about his death some years later.

I know it sounds like I'm using my writing as a therapeutic cleansing tool again, but that's not it at all. It's only that the more I write about it, the more I realize that maybe this was his destiny, that maybe his life should be fleeting if only to teach us something about our own mortality. Maybe, it's that we should appreciate this life we were given and not ever take it for granted.

However, until that fateful moment, no other 'flights of fancy' occurred that concerned my life, or none that I was aware of or can remember anyway. However, his relationship with Sheri did become very rocky and precarious about a year or so before he died, which, again, would shed further light on the instability of Bob and the problems he'd had as a young man.

My life would continue without much ado as I finally graduated from high school. Before graduating, I would get a part-time job working at Tony's Pizza during my senior year. However, once I graduated, I went full-time.

A year or so later, Dad and I would begin building my first home. A small A-frame just a stone's throw away from my parents. Some of my life's most stirring and incredible adventures would begin after moving into it when I was twenty.

But this will begin my next memoir, which is the real beginning of the craziness of my adult life. But I have one other story from my late teens concerning myself, my brother Tom, and his navy buddy, Doug, which is probably the actual incident that propelled me into my young adulthood.

Chapter 11

Independence—It Seems So Overrated

I worked at Tony's Pizza, a frozen food company, for eight months before graduating high school in 1981. Tony's was a large food manufacturer specializing in frozen pizza and various other frozen ethnic foods.

At the time, it produced a variety of pizza under the brand names of Tony's, Red Barron, and later on, Freschetta, along with various types of frozen Mexican cuisine, and I use the term 'cuisine' quite loosely. The company was, and still is, owned by Schwan's Sales Enterprises, you know ... the makers of Schwan's 'world-famous' ice cream and various other sundries.

The company was located in Salina, Kansas, a small city fifteen miles West of Solomon. Although it wasn't a large metropolis, it did have a 'staggering' population of about 40,000 people, which was about 25 times larger than Solomon and, therefore, quite impressive, or so I thought.

I'd believed Salina held more promise for me than Solomon as I wanted to grow beyond my boundaries and explore the world and not the one I already knew, so after graduating at eighteen, I moved there.

For me, Solomon had become a place to move from rather than grow old in; it was stagnant, and living there was suffocating me. I would eventually realize, however, it's not where you live but where you're capable of going that creates the allure of infinite possibilities to discover and experience the unknown.

This was my first real, full-time job—where I would work for nearly seventeen years. While there, I would meet many good friends, attend college, and find myself in many precarious situations.

In fact, the first and only time I ever felt a black man's hair was in the break room one day when my friend, John Peoples, and I were talking. Out of the freaking blue, I stood up and stated matter-of-factly, "John, I'm going to do something, and I don't want you to hate me or feel weird about it."

But before he could say a word, I began running my hands all over his head. What the hell do you think went through his head at that very minute ... nothing, apparently, because he didn't say a word. I know I shocked the crap right out of him, and I have to say, it felt pretty damn cool. It was really cushy—you know, spongy.

I would come to know a variety of people, of which some were interesting, and others were a bit ... well, let's just say, odd. I loved it there, and through the years, worked up through the ranks to learn many of the various systems and eventually became the second- and third-shift Microbiology laboratory lead.

I was making a fair wage but always knew I could and would do more, which I have. It's been about fifteen years since then, though, and from what I understand, the company has morphed from a fun and friendly, family-owned and oriented environment where both management and workers cared to a true corporate money-making establishment.

Maybe it's just the natural progression of things; as companies become large and established, the people who do the work become tools for the money-makers and the powers that be. You know … those who run the company tend to become wealthy and seemingly uncaring. It almost seems that if they can't make more money, they'd make no money at all.

Regardless, it truly was an enjoyable place to work for many people, especially the younger set, a place with heart and soul. I think now it's only a place for people to work to make some semblance of a living.

We've all seen it; it's known as the 'corporate world,' where it's usually only about the bottom line, and heart and soul are secondary, if they exist at all. So now my only question is, how wealthy does a man have to be before he's rich? And finally, I want you to know this is one of only a few tirades you will be subjected to, though I have many.

Ever since I began working at Tony's, and especially after graduating, I wanted to move to Salina because I was a young man who wanted to be independent; you know, to sow my wild oats, so to speak, and explore the world. However, I wasn't able to afford to live alone at the time. I knew I would need help with rent and bills because I didn't want to live in some old shack just to make ends meet, so my next step was to look for a roommate or two to help with the rent.

I only knew a few people from work at the time, though, and most of them already had, or were, roommates, or they just wanted to live alone. So, in my quest for a roomy, I eventually hooked up with my brother, Tom, and his friend, Tim Hinchey— aka Doug Paris.

I can say I certainly got my money's worth with these two yahoos. The lesson I learned with these two is how you really don't know someone until they've moved from your life … I'm, of course, speaking of Doug, which is how I will refer to him since it was the name I knew him by.

It began when Tom moved home after leaving the Navy, and Doug tagged along; why they moved back to Kansas, only God knows. Maybe Doug thought it was a good place to lie low; you know, low-key and quiet where you're generally out of the way. They had both landed jobs almost immediately working for El Dorado, an RV manufacturer in Minneapolis, Kansas.

These two were a pair, I tell ya, and although my brother was no saint by any stretch of the imagination, Doug was a real piece of work; a confused and on the lamb kind of guy. I eventually found out he wasn't who he professed to be, and although Tom knew who and what he was, he always kept Doug's secret—at least while Doug was around. A lot of bad decisions were made by Doug, and a lot more bad decisions were made to cover up the original bad decisions.

So, we found a duplex in Salina and moved into the Fox Run subdivision, located only a few blocks from Tony's. Fox Run was converted from Air Force housing when Schilling Air Force Base was still operating. They were remodeled duplex homes … affectionately known as 'garden' and 'town' homes, depending on the model. They were really quite nice, but with precious little insulation, the winter and summer electric bills were enormous.

Another drawback was that there were only two designs and about the same number of colors, so it was easy to mistake which house was yours if you came home late some night and were drunk. It could be a little confusing until you get used to the layout. And it was here that I cut my teeth messing with the law, which occurred in the late summer or early fall of 1981.

I had been visiting family and friends in Solomon one evening and was heading back home. I didn't drink much back then, only when I was partying or having a few beers at home with friends. So, I had been as sober as an out-of-wine Franciscan monk that night.

It was a good thing, too, because just after returning to Salina from Solomon, I was red-lighted by a police cruiser and was stopped. *No big deal,* I thought, as I wasn't speeding or drinking. I hadn't done anything that would warrant a ticket. *Maybe I have a headlight or a turn signal out*, I casually thought as I pulled over for the officer.

I rolled my window down as he walked up to my door. He then asked, "Your license, please?"

"Sure," I said and reached to get my wallet. As I handed it to him, I asked why he had stopped me.

Looking at my license, he stated matter-of-factly, "We've had a report of a hit-and-run involving a yellow Ford Pinto, which matches the description of your car, sir."

I remember thinking, *'Sir,' I ain't no Sir. I'm only eighteen years old.*

I looked at him and let out a little, "Huh? It wasn't my car, officer," I said in a slightly baffled tone, then added, "I just got back into town from Solomon."

He answered, "I don't know that sir, and won't know anything until we look at your car, Mr. McMillan."

I think this guy's serious ... then a little wave of uncertainty washed over me, and I became slightly nervous.

I immediately offered, "I can show you my car, officer."

To which he asked without hesitation or so much as a peep of an acknowledgment, "Would you please step out of the car, Mr. McMillan?"

Until this moment, I had been fairly calm, cool, and collected, but with his almost accusing tone, I became somewhat unnerved and a little disconcerted. I had never in my young adult life been approached by a cop before, let alone in such a serious manner; I'd never given them a reason to. The worst thing I'd done recently was to fart in the wrong place at the right time ... and that's a true story for yet another book.

I immediately complied with the officer's request and stepped out of the car. I then took the proactive approach and began showing him around my car. I sure as hell didn't want him to think for a single minute I was hiding anything.

So, we began our inspection, and just as we rounded the back of the car, I remembered something. It was something so damn nerve-racking I had to silently catch my breath as my heart jumped into my throat and began racing a million miles an hour. You know the feeling; it's like when you're just getting ready to head over the first drop on a really tall and fast roller coaster for the first time—you just don't know what to expect.

All of a sudden, my palms became cold and clammy. I instantly became silently horrified by what might happen should I start acting overly nervous, which would just lead to an emotional feedback loop, and then surely shit would hit the fan. If the cop noticed me going into an utter and complete total meltdown, which probably would have appeared like I was having a freaking cerebral hemorrhage, I would surely be caught. I just don't take stuff like this well—then or now.

I became absolutely dumbfounded. I braced myself and continued walking around inspecting the car, answering his questions with a simple nod or a "Yes sir" or "No sir." I tried keeping the answers and comments to an absolute minimum and on a need-to-know basis.

I don't know how I pulled it off, but I managed to stay composed just long enough to get completely around the car. He then pointed to the front door and gave me the go-ahead to get back inside, saying, "Please get into your car, Mr. McMillan." Feeling like a ton of bricks had been lifted off my chest, I turned from the cop and let out a long, slow sigh of relief under my breath. I think I actually heard the choir sing out a big 'Halleluiah' once I got back in the car.

He had kept my license during the ordeal, and just as he was handing it back to me, feeling confident, I mentioned there was another car like mine around town, only it was a hatchback, whereas mine was a two-door. He asked if I knew who owned it, to which I said, "No Sir," which I didn't. He then told me to drive carefully as he stepped back into his cruiser. I took off feeling relieved but with about half of my six trillion cerebral synapses firing simultaneously.

As I drove home, my mind was in a state of raging anger. I was a frigging nervous wreck. I was cursing Tom and Doug all the while and swore I was going to kick both of their asses the next time I saw them. Once I got to Fox Run, I drove straight to the back of the complex, where an empty field was located. I stopped on a deserted area of the road, then got out and opened the trunk.

From inside, I grabbed a large green duffle bag and headed out to the tree line about a hundred yards off into the field. I threw that fucking bag and all its contents into the ditch and never thought twice about it as I walked back to my car.

Fortunately for them, we didn't see each other till the next day when I had mostly calmed down, so I never gave them the 'What For' I'd planned the previous evening. But they didn't completely escape my wrath either.

You see, earlier in the evening, before I headed to Solomon, Tom and Doug had brought home a duffel bag full of pot, to which I proceeded to freak out when they showed it to me.

I screamed at them both, "You need to get rid of that shit now, and I mean *now*!" Of course, they were more than slightly miffed by my instant reaction and attitude toward their little 'windfall.' But I kept pressing on. "I don't want it in my house, you assholes!"

Tom immediately shot back, "Why the hell are you so pissed, Bird?"

"Why the hell am I pissed?" I repeated indignantly. "Because it's a bag full of pot, you brainiacs! That's why!" which was my final retort. I was sure that with these two, having a duffle full of pot around was an invitation to sure disaster—which it almost was.

I eventually calmed down, but only enough to allow them to take a couple of tokes of the stuff to see if it was any good. Why I didn't continue with my rant, I don't know, especially knowing if it were any good, they would keep it. But it was probably because I knew, like every other person in Kansas, that if you find marijuana growing wild in Kansas, it's probably no good ... that's why they call it K-weed or ditch weed.

They then dried enough to roll a doobie and take a few tokes. After a few minutes, they declared the stuff was crap and decided to trash it. But then they made an excuse for not being able to get rid of it, just then anyway.

Their 'reason' was because they were in a hurry. They were running late for a pool tournament at the bar and had to leave now. But, like a dipshit, I told them I would get rid of it on my way to Solomon. So, I threw it in the trunk of my car, and of course, out of sight, out of mind, and throughout the evening, I completely spaced it out ... well, at least until the freaking cop stopped me.

So, even though I didn't get busted, and it's actually quite funny today, you can see how I could never really get hooked on or deal drugs ... even though I'm certainly not innocent and have done them in my life. I never let it get the better of me when I did, and I haven't had anything to do with that scene in many years and will never mess with any of the crap again.

Had I gotten caught that night with 20 pounds of pot in the trunk of my car, I would have been shipped up the creek without a damn paddle. Even in the early 80s, it was a major crime to possess that much marijuana, even if it wasn't mine, which I could never have proved. So, it was actually a serious deal, and one for which I'm lucky, and thank God I didn't get caught.

That was the first big thing that happened to me on my first try at independence. And although we only lived together for about six months before Tom and Doug moved on, it was still quite a learning and nerve-racking experience. It wasn't all bad, though. I did find that I enjoyed living away from home, on my own, so to speak.

However, it wasn't until after they moved that I really had to question what these two were up to before moving back to Kansas, or at least what Doug was up to. Although this is more of a story for my brother's book, if he ever writes it, I will give just enough detail so that my story concerning what I've already written about these two will explain why they really were a couple of yahoos.

Not long after they moved, but before my next roommate, Kenny Houser, Bob's brother, moved in, I was paid a little visit by the fine men of the Salina Police Department. Or at least I think they were the police ... and from Salina. They weren't dressed like cops, more like detectives, but nevertheless, they asked a bunch of questions concerning Doug when they showed up at my door one morning.

When I answered the door, I was surprised to find two police officers looking for Tim Hinchey. I told them I didn't know Tim Hinchey, to which they replied, "He might also be known as 'Douglas Paris.'

"Really?" I asked rhetorically.

Then, knowing I could get into trouble if I said I didn't know anyone by that name, I explained that he had been my roommate but had moved out about a month ago. They asked if I knew where he went, to which I replied, "I don't have any idea; he just moved out one day before I got home." Which was true.

They were nice and not overly persistent, but they asked me to call them if I heard anything. But before leaving, I asked why they were looking for Doug. Of course, they wouldn't tell me because they weren't able to give out that information, so I let it go at that. It wasn't until some years later that Tom told me the real story about 'Doug.'

Apparently, just before leaving the Navy, Doug bought a car. However, he realized he couldn't afford it, so rather than letting it be repossessed, he decided to report it stolen and ditch it at a lake. If he reported it stolen, he could collect the money to pay the car off—but that never happened.

Tom had been following Doug to Green Mountain to ditch the car when he got the truck he was driving stuck in the mud. The next day, Doug and some other buddies were heading back to get the truck unstuck and finish the job but were stopped for speeding.

The cop must have known that the car had been reported stolen, so he moved Doug to the cruiser while he checked out the car and plates. His unfortunate move was not handcuffing Doug and leaving his nightstick in the front seat.

While the cop was standing with his back to them, Doug grabbed the club, stepped out, snuck up behind the cop, and began beating him with it. Apparently, the cop had called for backup because, within minutes, another cop was at the scene.

Doug didn't have time to get away, and they took him to jail and impounded the car. Doug was only required to stay in jail for a few days and was released on his own recognizance because of their very lenient point system in Washington State.

He never showed up for his trial, though. He decided to abscond and skipped town with Tom tagging along. So, in their infinite wisdom, the dingbats decided to go to Colorado to 'squat' on some land and grow marijuana.

While camping in the mountains of Walden County, Colorado, a fast, furious, freak snowstorm blew in on them. It was pretty brutal and way more than they could handle as campers, so they broke into a private cabin, which was located not too far from their campsite.

Later, after the snow stopped, they headed back down the mountain to get supplies from their camp. On their way back up, they met some cops but had time to stash some pot and a gun they had been carrying before they were taken into custody for breaking and entering.

They had to spend a week in jail waiting until the judge returned from vacation. They were charged with trespassing. Luckily, back then, there weren't computer systems or the internet as there is today, so the judge didn't realize that Doug was a fugitive.

Once they were released, they headed straight for Solomon and moved into my parents. Unbeknownst to anyone, just after landing in Kansas, Tom and Doug went to Topeka, where Doug scoured the state records of dead children that would be approximately his age at the time. He lifted the name and records of a Douglas Paris, which is the name by which I knew him, and not Timothy Hinchey, which was his real name.

He then applied for and received a new birth certificate, effectively giving him a new identity. When Tom told me this, he also explained that Doug (Tim) eventually gave himself up because he was tired of running.

So that's the thick and thin of my childhood and teens, and although I believe these were some pretty trying events in my life, especially the Jim incident, some of the most exciting events are yet to happen.

Epilogue

Well, my friend, we're now at that infamous point of the roller coaster ride known as the big drop. It's been an interesting ride getting here. I know it seemed slow at times when I was giving a little background about myself, the town, and my childhood homes. I felt it necessary to tell you a little about myself so you can better appreciate how and why these things sometimes happened. And, too, I wanted you to get to know me as a real person, not just a collection of 'episodes' from my life. But in my next book, I will push the limits as we careen down that big drop through the next part of my life—the young adult years.

We will be talking about me as an adult rather than as a child; as children, we get into trouble because sometimes we don't realize there can be, and usually are, consequences to our actions. However, as adults, especially young adults, we're most times completely aware of what we're doing, only many of us are too stupid to not do it ... whatever 'it' is. But that's what makes life exhilarating and risky all at once, especially during these particular years.

I also want to say that although some of those things I've done were because I was downright stupid, I very much tried to be a good guy regardless of the circumstance, and sometimes it was to no avail because ... well, let's face it, sometimes crap just happens, even to the best of us or even to us with the best intentions.

And, so as not to 'shock' you per se, some of the things I will be writing about concern things that some might find a little risqué and somewhat bizarre, but they're really only about a living and learning experience—my living and learning experience.

I won't be nearly as graphic about 'those' episodes as I was about my 'molestation,' but I don't have to be. The few events concerning sex really only concern sex as a secondary issue to the actual events that occurred, so it's really all good in that respect.

At the same time, however, I want to also hook you just a little with the expectation of reading about a person who's either done things or had things happen that most people would never dream of experiencing personally in their own lives. So, without further ado, here are a few highlights from the trials and tribulations that I call my life:

First, I will tell you about building my A-frame home in Solomon and the many suckass events while living there. I had begun hanging out with a group of friends from work, a good group, but was blindsided after being informed that one of those friends was gay and because he and I hung around a lot, in my mind, it was guilt by association, and therefore they thought I was gay as well.

I go on to tell of how he and I ended up in a very precarious situation at a party one night, nearly getting myself killed during an altercation that ensued. I then tell of another time when I caught this same person at a different party having 'relations' in the bedroom with a total scum bucket. I went berserk in front of everyone at the party only to have my girlfriend confront me and subsequently break up with me because I loathed him and his homosexuality ... and we all know what this stems from, don't we.

As time went on, I decided to rent the A-frame to Bob and Sheri so I could move back to Salina to live and party with another group of friends from work. This turned into a stocking situation after Sheri separates and Bob moves out.

After being separated for some time, Bob tried to again commit suicide, only this time damn near doing it right in front of her. Then, about four months later, he did commit suicide in my garage after recovering from his previous unsuccessful attempt, but it was under very odd circumstances how he did it and how he was found.

If that weren't enough, I had an accident a year later that nearly took my life but rather only maimed me for life. And during my nearly three months stay in the hospital, I came to a very serious realization about myself that would haunt me for years to come, but I would make peace with as I came to understand myself.

I later took a 13-year-old juvenile delinquent cousin into my home to help keep him from being taken from his family. No sooner than moving from Tennessee to Solomon did a 32-year-old neighbor bitch, who professed to be a witch, befriend him only to use him as her personal sex toy. And then, to top it all off, I nearly got thrown in jail for sexual abuse of a minor because Frankie lied to protect her ... this was most certainly just a wonderful and life-affirming experience. But this is only the tip of the iceberg as it concerns this young man. This is one hell of a story, and I aged 10 years in six months from the experience.

Although each of these stories are events that have occurred throughout my life, I will also write about personal things, things like the paranormal ... you know, ghosts, UFOs, and the like, and a few other 'odds' and ends as well—if you catch my drift. I have to sometimes think maybe Bob wasn't so given to flights of fancy after all. I just didn't want to try and explain myself during the telling of our story as friends together so many years ago, but rather give them their own relevance and due as they occurred.

These are only some of the many things I will be writing. However, I am keeping a few things up my sleeve to give you a few surprises, which I'm sure you will enjoy as well.

Finally, my sister-in-law, Tina, texted me a little blurb that Chris wanted me to see. It's funny as hell (I don't really know how funny hell is, but I feel I've visited it on more than one occasion). Here's how it goes:

"Insanity doesn't run through my family, oh no, it walks in, strolls through, and takes its time to get to know each and every one of us personally."

I'm sure many of us can relate to this at one time or another during this crazy thing we call life.

I hope you've enjoyed my book and that you'll enjoy my next one as much as I have writing it. So, my friend, until then, please be good, and be good at it. Talk to you soon and best wishes till then.

Your Friend,
J. Bryson McMillan.

www.ingramcontent.com/pod-product-compliance
Lightning Source LLC
Chambersburg PA
CBHW070704130626
46553CB00005B/1824